Yes, Pets Do Go To Heaven!

*How to Communicate with Pets in the Afterlife,
Understand Signs & Why You Will See Them Again*

Sophia Grace

Table of Contents

Introduction

My philosophy when it came to pets was much like that of having children: You got what you got, and you loved them unconditionally regardless of whatever their personalities or flaws turned out to be
—Gwen Cooper (Ingram, 2020).

I want you to know, if you have lost a pet, my heart goes out to you. I may not know you, but I understand deeply the love between a pet and their pet parent. The bond between an animal and its owner is indescribable. For any committed and loving pet owner, the quote above would not seem strange at all. Those who share deep bonds with their pets know that they have personalities. They seek and give affection, understand your tone and body language, as you learn to understand theirs. They know when you are sad or upset. Our pets care about us too. I think that any person who has never experienced this was not ready to have a pet. Pets are not shy to communicate their needs. If they are shy or afraid, it is possible that they have experienced trauma. They will need healing, perhaps rehabilitation, to become their natural, loving, caring, and spontaneous selves.

My friend, Louisa, and her husband Dave were traveling by car one day, and as they passed underneath a bridge, they saw a kitten lying next to the road. Her husband stopped the car and they carefully picked up the kitten. She was clearly hurt. She was a mess. She hissed and scratched, trying to get away. They already had other pets, but they couldn't leave her there. They had to do something to help her. Louisa had a small blanket in the trunk, so they carefully wrapped the kitten in the blanket and took her to the vet. The vet examined her and told Louisa and Dave that the kitten was not only neglected but abused also.

He said that he could not save her leg. It seemed that a car ran over it. The vet explained that an operation to amputate her leg and to nurse her back to health would be expensive and that the best solution would be to put her down. But Louisa and Dave would not hear of it. Although they were not particularly rich, they were adamant that the kitten would be saved. The vet then said that he couldn't keep her, and it was unlikely that someone would adopt her. Louisa smiled and said, *No worries. She already has a home.* They filled out the proper documentation and named the kitten *Patsy*.

The kitten was operated on, and her right hind leg was amputated. She was still frantic and wild. When she was well enough, Louisa and Dave took her home. She was introduced to the other pets who showed a lot of interest. Patsy was frightened and hid wherever she could find a place. Her new parents were patient and gentle. Days went by and Patsy started to show signs of acceptance. Not long after that, Patsy willingly came to them, looking for attention. About a year later, Patsy transformed into the queen of the house. Since then, she walks around with her three legs as if she owns the entire house! Today, she craves more attention than any of the other pets. I commented on how wonderfully she had healed, physically and mentally. Louisa replied, *In many ways, she healed us more.*

How could something this beautiful be temporary? We are all—animals and humans—spirits living in temporary bodies. Why would creation be filled with such awe and splendor be given to us, simply to be taken away again? I believe that all this glory is a glimpse of Paradise. It is a taste of what awaits us in the world after this one. A loving bond that is so strong that it can be compared to what we feel for other people, or children, cannot simply disappear. It must be everlasting in eternity. There must be a promise that we will be reunited with our pets.

But is this just an empty hopeful thought? Not quite. In this book, *Yes, Pets Do Go to Heaven!* we will discuss the souls of animals, see the perspective of people in ancient times, and discover revelations leading to irrefutable proof that our pets have never left us, and neither will they. Their energy lingers, not as a floating oblivious mist or as a shadow against the wall, but a sentient presence, a familiar being who once shared a life with us, who understands us and wants us to be aware of their presence. We will peer into the afterlife, look at true accounts from credible witnesses, and rest in the knowledge that our pets will always love us and that we never need to stop loving them.

Pet owners often have to make difficult choices. *Do I let my pet leave the physical realm? Should I keep them around, even if they are suffering? Was I too quick to make a decision?* Losing a pet is a traumatic experience, whether the pet was ill, in an accident, or had to be put to sleep. It tears the heart apart in unimaginable ways. Some people mourn the loss of their pets by celebrating them, others in quiet remembrance. Whatever you do, never feel embarrassed for mourning your pet. Pets mourn owners who have passed too. Why should it be any different? Still, we have hope we can hold on to. We can rest in the knowledge that our pets stay with us, wanting us to know they are here.

You may wonder how some people can celebrate when their pets have passed. They are not celebrating the passing, but the pet. These people share their gratitude for having the opportunity to spend time with their pets. Of course, there will be sadness and grief. But think about this—if your loved ones had lost you, would you want them to remain in that dark pit that comes with loss? No, you would want them to heal and recover. You would want to see them happy again. Your pets want the same.

Does this mean that we should stop missing our pets? Not at all. This kind of loss wounds us deeply. Although the wounds may heal, there will always be a scar. That scar is the reminder of our time spent together. It is a space that will never be filled by anything else. But that's okay. You can use that space and fill it with the celebrations and memories of your pet, telling stories of your time together, remembering and harboring your love for them. Because although they are no longer in the physical realm, you can keep loving them for eternity. That is what love is—it never fades.

We will talk about tools you can use to communicate with your pet, finally finding the peace and contentment you desire. You, as the owner of your pet, knew your pet better than anyone. Your pet is aware of this. They know that you made choices, although being tough, in their best interest. The love shared between pets and their owners is unconditional. Neither pets nor their owners need to prove themselves to be loved.

For this reason, you need to become sensitive to your surroundings. You need to fine-tune your senses to become aware of your pet's presence and to notice the signs left by them. Their attempts at communication are there, it's just that most people never notice. If you want to notice and learn how to focus your attention on things mostly unseen, then this book is for you. You have always been the world to your pet, which is something that will not change. Only now, after your pet's passing, they are no longer limited to the physical realm. They have passed to a higher plane of existence, no longer bound to earth. But, although they are uplifted, their personalities stay the same.

How often have you experienced feeling sad or upset, and noticed changes in your pets' behavior? They know when we are feeling down. They become intently focused on us, trying to understand what is going on, but more than that, trying hard to make us understand that they are here for us. They will do anything to let their attempts at comfort come across. What great love this is! How can it be temporary? As is proven by the love shared between us and Divinity, love is a power that will never cease to exist. Love has the power to carry messages across in this life and from the world beyond ours.

As much as you were your pets' protector, they want to be yours. They know when you think of them. They are aware when you look at photos and watch videos of your time together. The love between you and your pets has bound you together forever. Come on

5

this journey with me, and together we will find ways to reconnect with your pets that have passed. All intelligent life understands love and grief. Your pets want to help you heal. They want to communicate with you. All you need to do is listen.

Chapter 1

Is My Pet's Soul Eternal?

Animals share with us the privilege of having a soul
—Pythagoras (Ingram, 2020).

Irst of all, let's answer the burning question: do animals have souls? We can answer this question by looking at our own souls. The human soul consists of three attributes—our will, intellect, and emotions. These qualities set us apart from other objects in the physical spectrum. The human will is displayed from a young age. For example, a toddler wanting a toy in a department store. They can make quite a ruckus with parents wanting to hide under the shelves sometimes. Intellect can also be seen from an early age. A baby understands your tone of voice and can either feel uneasy or calm. Emotions too can be seen when the baby is a few months old. What a beautiful day the first time a baby laughs!

Let's consider animals. We can determine that animals have souls with one simple example: a dog demanding attention from their owner. Will is at play here, as the dog *wants* attention—it is the dog's will to try and get attention from their owner. Intellect is also clearly visible: the dog *knows* that they can get attention if they demand it.

That is proof of cognitive ability. Finally, we can see that the dog must have a sense of emotion. Why else would the dog demand attention? They want to *experience* the attention of their owner to *feel* good and loved. The dog is just an example. We can see similar behaviors in cats, birds, horses, cows, and more. Elephants grieve the loss of one of their herd. That is a powerful display of animal emotion and intellect.

Now that we have determined that animals do indeed have souls, just like us, are their souls eternal like ours? In this chapter, we will go in search of answers.

What the Ancients Believed

According to Whitney Hopler (2019), scholars of ancient texts and afterlife experts agree that animals do have eternal souls. An animal does not simply cease to exist at some point. Not only do pets have the chance to join their owners in the afterlife, but every animal that has ever existed, even when they had no relationship with humans, has their place in the eternal Paradise. People having animals as companions is not a brand-new concept. The practice possibly dates back 32,000 years. These animal-human relationships have a positive influence on us, both physically and psychologically. This means that we were always supposed to bond with animals. They are, just like us, on earth for a reason.

No matter what faith you practice or what you believe in, all cultures and religions share accounts of creation. God, the Great Spirit, the Divine Being, whatever we believe, created the universe in all of its splendor. Nature and animals were created with mankind as the crown of creation. Animals were very important in many ancient religions. A lot of the Egyptian hieroglyphs that are identified and understood today refer to animals. In fact, many animals were revered and worshiped as deities. A large variety of animals were kept as pets by ancient Egyptians, not just cats and dogs, although cats were mostly kept as pets. This ancient civilization had strong bonds with their pets and cared for them deeply. Egyptians did not view themselves as superior to animals, but rather that animals were their equals.

The Egyptians loved their cats but also revered them as sacred since they were linked to Bastet. She was believed to be the goddess of childbirth, women's secrets, domesticity, fertility, and cats. She specialized in protecting, especially women and children, against diseases, and also protected their homes from evil spirits. Isn't that wonderful? Feeling the need to be protected from evil spirits indicates that they, just like all other religions and cultures, were aware of a realm beyond our own.

Loving to have cats as pets did not mean that dogs had no place. Dogs were also popular pets but also had their purpose in the military or police, or hunting. Herodotus, a Greek historian, noted that when a cat passed away, the entire household shaved their eyebrows. When a dog passed away, the household shaved their entire bodies (Joe, n.d.). Dogs were associated with the god Anubis, who was believed to accompany souls to the Hall of Truth. He was also believed to have presided over the process of mummification. Why was mummification performed? The Egyptians believed that the body

9

needed to be preserved for the afterlife. Again, we find proof that they were aware that souls are eternal and had rituals and practices accordingly.

Similar to ancient Egyptian belief, we see in Hinduism that they have also considered animals to have souls, and still do to this day. These souls are subject to physical and spiritual evolution. Because the higher realities of nature do not exist in them, they have limited cognitive capacity, lacking abilities such as ego, intelligence, and speech. Even so, it is believed that animals share the same consciousness as humans when it comes to the soul. There are other religions, such as Buddhism and Jainism, that share many of the same beliefs when it comes to animal spirits.

According to the Hindu Puranas, there are exceptions to limited cognitive capacity, such as when a person deliberately is reborn as an animal, if a god is born as an animal, normally associated with some purpose, or if an animal is born as part of a celestial event. Because of this and that animals are believed to be in the same cycle of death and rebirth as humans, they must be respected and allowed a chance to evolve. Laws were created to suggest how animals must be treated. Animal and human souls are seen as equal and no harm should be done to any animal. Should an animal be harmed by a human, it would mean that such a person is interfering with the animal's normal spiritual evolution which is something important and sacred in Hinduism.

It is believed that any kindness shown to an animal would bring about a great reward in the afterlife to the person showing the kindness. In the Puranas, it is also stated that gods may take the form of an animal to test their devotees in how they would treat the *animal*. It is clear that Hinduism holds great reverence for the spiritual plane. It is believed that animals have their own language which can only be understood by gods and celestial beings.

The ancient Greeks also believed in reincarnation, that the soul leaves the body when passing away, entering another physical body at the time of birth. They believed that animals and humans both shared the cycle of regeneration. They believed that the soul is an essential part of life that is present in both animals and humans. Harming an animal was considered equal to harming a member of your own family. What an amazing insight! I think it is safe to say that animal lovers feel the same way.

The Native American belief is that everything has a spirit. They regard animals not as inferior, but as people. Therefore, they have great reverence for nature, especially animals. It is believed that animals were involved in creation and that there are dogs that lead the souls of those who had passed to the afterlife. They believe that there are both practical and spiritual relationships between humans and animals. They also believe that whenever a person or animal enters the afterlife, they continue in the cycle of reincarnation.

The ancient Islam belief that humans and animals possess souls stands to this day. The Qur'an states that when you enter Heaven, you can have anything you want. This would mean that if you wanted your pets to be with you, they would be. I believe that people's senses have dulled because of technology and the rushed way people live their lives. In ancient times there were no such distractions. It was easier for people to get in touch with the spiritual realm, adding to

11

their awareness. This is why people who seek enlightenment have to find a place of absolute calm and peace, removed from the distractions of technology and being rushed. This is where they experience the Divine.

A Holy Declaration

Scholars and others who play significant roles in Judaism and Christianity are divided about the thought that animals have souls. Some believe that animal spirits, just like humans, continue to exist for eternity, while others say that animals simply cease to exist when they pass. The latter are probably those who have never had a pet. I'm not saying this lightly. Having a pet changes you. It changes your perspective and beliefs about animals. Some think because humans were given dominion over animals, animals are inferior. They lack the understanding that animals have emotions, cognitive ability, and are able to communicate. How can anything without a soul have these capabilities?

When our pets pass away, do we not mourn them as we would a family member or one of our children? Why do we mourn our pets? It is because we form a loving bond with them. We get to know our pets, their personalities, habits, likes, and dislikes. How can anyone think that their pet has no soul? This is why, when a pet passes, you cannot simply *replace* them as you would a television set or a bicycle. Although we call ourselves pet owners, we don't really *own* pets. It goes both ways. Our pets own us just as much as we own them. Owning something implies that you have a responsibility to take care of it. With pets, it goes far beyond that. We don't simply take care of our pets—we love, cherish, and nurture them.

As time goes by and research is done with animals as subjects, the idea that animals have souls is accepted by more people. For example, it is found that whales and dolphins use intricate language and can communicate without difficulty. Gorillas can form sentences by learning to use sign language. Many animals show high levels of intelligence. I am sure that you as a pet owner have witnessed your pet's intelligence countless times. You understand when your pet is asking for food, to go outside, or for you to give them affection. How would you know these things? Your pet is communicating with you, which means they have an understanding of what to do to get certain responses.

It is interesting to note that the prophet Isaiah wrote something about a new world that waits, a world where *the wolf and the lamb will feed together, and the lion will eat straw like the ox* (Isaiah 65:25 NIV). What makes it interesting is that this is very similar to the account of the Garden of Eden. *...to all the beasts of the earth and all the birds in the sky and all the creatures that move along the ground—everything that has the breath of life in it—I give every green plant for food* (Genesis 1:30, NIV). In both accounts, no animals were harmed or would harm each other. As the Garden of Eden is understood as the first Paradise, it would mean that this Paradise would be restored, where no harm would come to any animal. This also means that animals will live in the new Paradise—in Heaven. This is exciting!

In September of 2020, Pope Francis made a declaration that all of mankind must live in harmony with nature and all of Creation. He reminded us that all of Creation will become part of the Eternal Sabbath (which is Heaven). He stated that mankind and nature with all of her creatures live an inter-relational existence. We must love, honor, and cherish Creation as we do God. He made it clear that he believed in the existence of animals in the afterlife. The Italian newspaper *Corriere Della Sera* reported on this beautiful message. They included a quote from Pope Paul VI, telling the story of a young boy who was mourning the loss of his beloved pet. Pope Paul VI said to the boy, *One day we will see our animals in the eternity of Christ* (Abercrombie, 2014). What a comforting message and beautiful statement! Having the position of Pope, neither Pope Francis nor Pope Paul VI would make these statements lightly. They must surely believe what they are saying.

What would Creation be without its creatures? Therefore, when Pope Francis declared that *all* of Creation would enter the Eternal Sabbath, it must include animals. He further stated that we must exist with Creation in vocation and love. Animals should not simply be our property but must be respected and cared for. Since the Roman Catholic Church is also divided by the question of whether animals have immortal souls, let's take a look at what the Bible says.

First of all, animals did not come into existence by chance. Not only the Bible, but several other ancient texts describe the creation of nature and man, which included animals. According to the Bible, God looked at every aspect of Creation and said that it was good. This refers to Creation in its totality, which includes animals. Why then, if there is a promise of a new Creation, would animals simply cease to exist? Except for animals being in Heaven, God has a great fondness for animals, according to the Bible.

How do you feel about something you've created, such as a painting, a poem you've written, or maybe a house that you have restored? You feel immense pride and joy. Since we are created in God's image, why would He not feel the same about His Creation? We can see in Matthew 10:29-31 that God is watchful over animals and birds. He knows when a sparrow falls to the ground. Yes, the verse is about humans being of higher importance, yet, animals are still important enough to God that He is moved by the passing of one of His creatures.

God's loving care toward animals is displayed when He spoke to Jonah about his concern toward both the people and the animals (Jonah 4:11). God made it clear that He not only wanted to save the people but the animals as well. I'm sure we are all familiar with the story of Noah. However, did you ever consider how it came to be that the animals entered the ark? The only explanation is that God told them to board the ark. This would indicate a relationship between God and animals. Another beautiful example is when God told the ravens to take care of Elijah while he was at the river Jordan, by bringing him food (1 Kings 17:4-6).

In Job 39:6, God indicates that every animal was created for a purpose and placed in creation to fulfill their part. We can read in Psalm 148 that the psalmist calls on various kinds of animals to bring praise to God. Then, contrary to the belief of many theologians, clergy, and others, animals have the capacity to praise and worship God. God has a more intimate relationship with animals than many people expect. I think it is that some people have become so arrogant as to think we are so special that no other living being can compare to the divine favor we may find.

Yet God has created each animal with such careful detail that they have been able to exist for millions of years. If you were to place such care and detail into something you have created, would you decide that it would someday simply not exist anymore? I seriously doubt it. Animals are also in touch with the spiritual realm. Is this just a wild opinion I'm throwing around? Hardly. As I have aided many people with their loss of either friends, family members, or pets, I've had a fair share of seeing things with my own eyes. I've seen animals react to things that we cannot see. Animals would stare at walls, or sniff at something in mid-air that *wasn't there*. Of course, for them there is something there, we just don't see it.

If I told you that animals can see angels, would you believe me? When you read the part in Numbers 22:21-33, you can see that Balaam's donkey saw the angel of the Lord standing in the way. The donkey did everything to protect Balaam, even after he was beaten three times. Only the third time Balaam beat his donkey did God allow for the donkey to speak. The Bible never mentions that God allowed the donkey to see the angel of the Lord, which means that it was something the donkey could do anyway. Therefore, animals can see angels. I'm not saying *all* animals can, the Bible doesn't specify, but we can say for sure that some animals do. This indicates a connection between animals and the spirit world, even before they pass on to eternity.

Are My Pets in Paradise?

King Solomon speaks to the arrogance of people, stating that man and animal share the same destinies. In Ecclesiastes 3:21 he writes: *Who knows if the human spirit rises upward and if the spirit of the animal goes down into the earth?* In this part, he states that animals do have spirits, and are therefore eternal. Who of us would dare challenge a king who received wisdom as a gift from God? There are countless testimonies of people who claimed to have seen the afterlife, or Heaven and have made some amazing and controversial statements. Many of them claimed to have seen animals in Heaven.

As I am a spiritual advisor, I help people deal with the loss of a loved one or a pet. I teach them skills to communicate and recognize messages and signs that may have been left by their pets or loved ones. Several people are famous for helping others connect specifically with their pets who had passed. Some of these pet psychics, as they call themselves, can communicate with pets in this world and also in life hereafter. These pet psychics include people such as Shirley Scott, Latifa Meena, Nancy Mello, Lisa Holm, Carrie Kenady, and Danielle MacKinnon.

Let's talk about Danielle MacKinnon. She is a sensitive, pet psychic, and animal whisperer who holds workshops where she teaches people the skills to understand, communicate, and interpret messages and dreams from their pets. Similar to what I do, she works with people and teaches them about things that she has experienced personally. Many people come to her after the loss of a beloved pet, seeking comfort and healing. To ensure successful communication,

Danielle wants no information from those who come to her. She wants to hear directly from the pets who have passed. She says that being fed information interferes with the animal's voice, and she prefers that the messages are pure and unfiltered.

During these sessions, many people have asked what Heaven is like for their pets. Some refer to it as the afterlife, the next world, or the Rainbow Bridge, but whatever people prefer, it refers to the same plane of existence. Danielle says that different animals describe Heaven in different ways. For example, a dog may speak of endless fields where they can run, several puddles of mud, and soft green grass they can roll on. A cat may speak of places where they can lay and look at the other animals, a warm sunny glow all day long, and peace as they love it most. Some may say that these animals are either not in the same place, or that Danielle is not telling the truth (MacKinnon, 2019).

But think about it—what would your pet's Heaven be like? Would your dog, cat, parakeet, goldfish, or bearded dragon love the same things? They wouldn't, therefore Heaven would be different for each of them. It is the same place, but Heaven caters to every animal's loves and likes. Understand that our human minds will not be able to grasp the complexity of an eternal place such as Heaven, at least not while we are still in our physical form. Animals would all be able to exist in perfect harmony, just like it was meant to be, as it was in the Garden of Eden when the earth was fresh and new.

After transitioning to the spiritual realm, we can create with our thoughts and memories. We can create what we want, as long as it makes us feel happy and complete. The same goes for animals. In the afterlife, animals won't be limited as they are no longer bound to physical bodies that must adhere to the earthly laws of nature. This means that an animal's cognitive ability expands drastically, freeing them from the limitations they had to exist with on earth. While our pets are still with us, we can already determine their likes and dislikes. We get to learn what they love to do. Your dog, for example, may love to go on walks with you or go for a swim. Your cat may love laying on your lap or playing with strings and feathers. Now imagine the possibilities if your pets could create their own perfect place of happiness.

Not only will our and our pets' bodies be without limitation, but so will the activities we engage in. Imagine the most fun your pet could ever have and multiply it with a hundred. Even then what you imagine will not come close to what our pets who have passed are experiencing. Many people who communicate with loved ones or pets that have transitioned say that their loved ones speak of brilliant light, warmth, vivid colors that we have never seen on earth and a never-ending feeling of love and peace. It is not a place filled with clouds where people walk around with white robes all day. It is as physical as earth, if not even more so. Our world may eventually come to an end, but the world beyond the veil will never cease to exist, therefore making it more real than the physical plane.

Although there are houses in the spirit world, nature is vast and more magnificent than you can imagine. Many people testify of seeing or being aware of all kinds of animals in the afterlife. Although they are not the same, as they are now without limit, they are still recognized as animals. You may be worried that your pet won't be the same and will be unrecognizable. Don't worry about that. On earth, you have connected with your pet both physically and spiritually. When you are in Heaven, you will recognize your pet as you will remember the feel of their spirit, as they will yours.

Choo Thomas (2003) wrote that she saw a great number of animals playing together on what she called *animal mountain*. She described Heaven as a place of beauty, unlike anything any of us had ever seen on earth. All of the animals were happy, healthy, and radiant with love. That sounds like Heaven to me!

Halfway to Heaven

Doctor John Lerma specialized in working with terminally ill patients. One of his patients was an elderly lady, Mildred. She was 82 years old and diagnosed with multiple viscera, ovarian cancer, and widespread metastasis to the lungs and bones. She claimed to have been visited by multiple angelic beings, of which some had shown her visions of Heaven. In one such vision, she saw nature in its full glory and children playing amongst a multitude of animals and birds. People were assigned to look after the older people, who they called *sitters*. One day one of these sitters saw a beautiful lady dressed in an old nurse's uniform, talking to Mildred. She just stood there and watched them talking. When the beautiful woman was leaving, the sitter wanted to know what they were talking about. As she reached out to touch the woman's arm, her hand went straight through.

She then saw the woman walk into the room next to Mildred's, where another patient was being taken care of, Joseph. The sitter asked Mildred who she was talking to, to which Mildred replied that it was an angel. The sitter reported the incident to Doctor Lerma. When Doctor Lerma went to Joseph's room, he asked Joseph about the beautiful woman in old nurse's clothes. Joseph smiled and said that she was there with him and that she prayed with him. He also said that she was an angel. Doctor Lerma later testified that staff members reported hearing sounds coming from some of the rooms, such as laughter or animal sounds. This means that the staff members were able to hear visions that were shown to the terminally ill patients.

For the next testimony, we'll call the young lady *Jenny*. Jenny was a college student and in the middle of stressful exams. Because of this, she hardly slept and didn't eat well. Her boyfriend and a friend came to her house as she decided to take a quick break. Suddenly she lost her vision due to her blood pressure rapidly falling. She then fainted. Her boyfriend and the other friend rushed her to a hospital. They noticed that Jenny was having seizures. After being a while at the hospital, Jenny recovered. She had experienced something spectacular but decided to keep it to herself.

After she had blacked out she had the sensation that she was flying. Then she saw it—it was beautiful, which she described as a white enamel canyon. She saw trees and a crystal clear stream below. She realized that she was flying on the back of a giant bird. Everything was radiating the purest white light, all etched in brilliant and beautiful colors. She was aware of the colorful feathers below her. Jenny had the sensation that she and the bird were as one. Wherever or however she wanted to fly, the bird was in sync with her. She heard a voice behind her, calling her back. She didn't want to go back. The destination was up ahead, so she wanted to travel as quickly as possible to get there. Suddenly Jenny woke up. She explained that this place she saw, or at least a vision of it, this Heaven was more real than our world. She felt that the world she returned to was temporary, but the world she had witnessed was eternal, even though physical matter did not exist.

Cynthia was diagnosed with non-compaction ventricular cardiomyopathy, which is a heart defect. During her son's rehearsal dinner, Cynthia was not feeling all too well. She decided to take a beta-blocker as a precaution. But before she could, she collapsed. At that moment she knew she was dying. Although she expected to be afraid, she did not feel any fear. Instead, she felt calm and at peace. A white light enveloped her as well as a comforting breeze. Cynthia felt like she did not have a body, nor the need for one. Then a different sensation overcame her—she felt connected to the universe and all life. She understood that most humans only care for themselves, while the spirits of the animals are just as connected to us as we are connected to each other.

As a young boy, John Davis was riding one of his parents' mopeds. As he turned a corner, there was a squirrel in the road. John swerved in an attempt to miss the squirrel but ended up crashing right into a tree. This caused injury to the extent that he needed surgery to reattach the tendons to the bones in his right hand. He was quite nervous as this was his first operation. He was given an anesthetic and remembers feeling it coursing through his body. But something went wrong—John was allergic to this type of anesthesia. The moment it reached his heart, it stopped beating.

John remembers opening his eyes and seeing a magnificent white marble building. Someone was standing next to him, yet he never saw this person. The person continually spoke to him. First, John was told to look down a tunnel, which seemed to be carved from this brilliant white marble. He saw planets, moons, suns, and galaxies. The person explained to John that this was the doorway where all people entered who had passed away. Although it was not explained to John, he knew that this *person* was his spirit guide. Many people testify of having spirit guides when they have near-death experiences or have visions of the afterlife.

Next, the guide told John to look down the second tunnel. He saw a man walking, then grabbed his chest and fell to the ground. The guide explained that the man was having a heart attack and that he would be joining them soon. Sure enough, John suddenly saw the man in the great marble building. A young woman approached the man, who seemed to be in his eighties. John's guide explained that the woman is the old man's guide, helping him to transition. As the woman was speaking to the old man, his face began to change. He became younger and younger until he was no older than his late twenties or early thirties.

The man smiled and walked down some stairs into a garden. John described the garden as absolutely beautiful, somehow seeming to be alive, but other than that, there are no words to describe it. The man met people there, whom the guide explained were loved ones that had crossed over years before. The guide then took John to mountains filled with trees and green grass. Suddenly John saw animals come running down the hills of the mountain. As he stood there in amazement, his guide explained that all animals that were ever loved on earth wait in this place for the moment their people arrive. Then they run to greet them.

John was overwhelmed. He was aware of an awesome feeling of happiness and love. All the animals played with each other. He then saw two of his dogs and two of his cats who had passed come running. John's guide then took him to a field. As they were standing there, they were approached by a man who shone so bright that John could not make out any features. The man lifted his hands and told John to tell the world that *there is no death*. At that moment, John woke up. He saw the amazement in the eyes of the doctors who were standing over him. One exclaimed that John was alive. John had died and was gone for six minutes. John said that it did not feel like he was gone only for six minutes. The time he spent in Heaven felt like hours.

When Colton Burpo was four years old, he had a near-death experience while being operated on. He had trouble with his appendix. Colton described Heaven as being a beautiful place with lots of gardens. He also described meeting his grandfather who he has never met, as his grandfather died before Colton was born. More astoundingly, Colton told his parents that he met his sister. This was something his parents kept secret from him—before Colton was born, his mother had suffered a miscarriage. When his parents asked him who his sister was, he answered that she had passed away while she was still in his mommy's tummy. Goosebumps!

Colton also said that he saw many animals in Heaven, including pets. He was playing with some random dogs, without knowing who they were attached to. Although he was four years old, Colton said that he saw most animals that are on earth in Heaven. He even described seeing Jesus ride on a rainbow-colored horse. There were skeptics to his story, but Colton was able to give detailed accounts of how he was operated on, and what his parents did while he was looking down from Heaven. His parents were in separate parts of the hospital at one point, and Colton was able to tell them what they both were doing, also what they were saying.

A few things are clear from all these testimonies—there are animals in the afterlife, which means animals do have eternal souls, our pets are waiting for us to come and get them the moment we arrive in Paradise, and we can find comfort and begin our process of healing, knowing that we will one day be reunited with our beloved pets again. Many of us struggle with guilt concerning decisions we had to make on behalf of our pets. Did I wait too long? Should I have waited longer? Did I cause unnecessary pain? I can tell you honestly, from all the things that I have learned, and from personal experience, these things do not matter anymore. As our pets leave their earthly bodies and transition into the spirit world, every pain is forgotten. They exist in perfect love and happiness. There is no resentment. They don't think about pain anymore. All they think about is us. Your pets' only concern is that they will see you again.

Chapter 2

Messages from Beyond the Veil

Grief is like the ocean; it comes on waves ebbing and flowing.
Sometimes the water is calm, and sometimes it is overwhelming. All
we can do is learn to swim
—Vicki Harrison (Hollister, 2018).

The Grieving Heart

I think that pet psychics and communicators are underrated. Too many people face the loss of their pet alone, not knowing what to expect or what is expected of them. For someone who doesn't have anyone to guide or help them, the loss of a pet can be overwhelming and devastating. Some people believe that pets aren't to be mourned, but these are mostly people who have never had any pets. They may say something like *Just get another cat*, or *Don't worry, there are plenty of other dogs you can adopt*. Have you ever encountered such comments? We may feel disbelief and anger at such comments, but keep in mind that these people are ignorant, often not by their own choice, but just due to the lack of having an intimate relationship with a companion animal.

The bond we have with animals is different for every person. The bond you have with your dog will likely not be the same as mine. We connect in different ways, and some methods that one person uses will not necessarily work for the next person. This is also because animals have their own personalities. Dogs, cats, birds, and any other pet you can think of, vary in personalities even among their own species. No two dogs, cats, or birds are the same. Just as we would cater to the differences in personality in our children, we do for our pets. It is sad to say that some people who own animals never take the time to learn about their pets' personalities. I think it is time that we as pet owners reach out and teach the world about this special opportunity—let them see and understand that they can have a beautiful and soulful connection with their pets.

Our past experiences and relationships with other people may affect how we treat our pets. If a person is not used to getting attached to another person, they may find it hard to have an attachment relationship with their pets. However, instead of passing judgment, we should make every effort to help them get there.

When we see to it that our bonds are strong, the relationship we have with our pets is so powerful that your pet will return to your home even after taking a stroll outside. It is not mere *instinct* that brings them back, it is their love for you. This relationship benefits both parties, humans and animals alike. It can relieve stress and improve overall health for both the animal and the human. This scenario is both beautiful and painful. When your pet grows older or has become ill to the extent that they cannot be cured, you know that your time together is almost coming to an end. This can cause emotional, mental, and physical pain.

There are many ways we can lose our pets. It may be sudden, such as in an accident. Or it may be because of old age and deterioration. Some pets leave us because of an incurable disease. I know one thing, from experience—there is no way of losing a pet that makes it easier than the other. It doesn't matter if you had more time or if you could plan your pet's passing, it is equally painful. This is why I would never say to someone who lost a pet something such as *At least you had more time together*, or *Your pet is in a better place*. Losing a pet leaves an indescribable void. You have all this love you want to share, but no one to give it to. It frustrates and sometimes infuriates.

As we are all unique individuals, our grief is also very personal and unique. As people do not experience grief the same, we cannot expect them to behave as we think is appropriate. We have to let every person grieve in their own way, and as such, allow ourselves to grieve in whatever way we see fit. In the grieving process, we should not judge others or let ourselves be judged. Crying is a normal part of the grieving process, but if a person is not crying, never think that they are not grieving. Other things that may occur during the grieving process are lacking concentration, losing your appetite, diarrhea, vomiting, insomnia, and becoming withdrawn. I need to mention all of this, as many people do not know that these things are normal while grieving.

Some people experience anger after the passing of their pet. Most people don't show this anger to others, as they were taught that being angry is an inappropriate emotion. But then how do they deal with it? Many project this anger on other people, in such cases you may witness an unexpected outburst over the tiniest of things. The subject of the outburst is not what is before you, but rather in the subconscious mind of the person who had lost their pet. If the person is unable to direct their anger on situations or people, they project the anger on themselves. The anger then turns into guilt. As people find it difficult to admit their guilt to others, it becomes an invisible burden that can be destructive to mental health.

There is a wide variety of emotions that can be experienced after the passing of a beloved pet. You should never feel embarrassed about these emotions. Any pet lover can attest to that.

Other emotions that are experienced can include sadness, sorrow, or depression. Depression is, however, more than just an emotion. It is a state of the mind which is difficult to escape from. Yet, although difficult, it is possible to heal from depression. There may also be mental symptoms accompanying grief, such as blame-shifting. This happens when a person cannot accept the passing of their pet and find a need to give reason to the passing, especially in placing blame. They may accuse the veterinarian of *not doing enough* or *taking too long*. Perhaps they accuse their partner and blame them for the passing of their pet.

Although painful and hard to deal with, when this happens, remember that this phase is temporary and that the person who is suffering emotionally does not mean or believe anything they are saying. It is just a way for them to try and deal with the situation. When a person is told that their pet has passed away and they are in denial of it, don't force the truth on them. Denial occurs when a person's mind would not be able to bear the full weight of the truth, namely that their pet has passed away, at one moment. They need time to process it, where denial is a strong coping mechanism for the mind to keep functioning as it should. If a person has to make difficult decisions while in the denial stage, be patient. Give them time and room to think and process.

Some people struggle more to cope with losing a pet, therefore becoming dependent and overly attached to other people. For example, when a child loses a pet, they may appear needy and clingy. Allow them this, as they need the emotional support to keep functioning. If the pet required a lot of care and special attention and suddenly passed, it can leave a giant void in their caregiver's life. It can be devastating to a person who took care of their pet 24/7, to suddenly have no pet to care for.

As I said earlier in this section, every person grieves differently. You may have experienced some of the symptoms mentioned in this section and not the others. This section is also meant for you to know how to treat others when they have lost their pets. Don't judge and never criticize someone's grieving process. Just let them understand that you are there to support them with love and compassion. In the same way, if you need support due to the loss of a beloved pet, don't hesitate to find a support system. Even when your pet is diagnosed with a terminal illness, reach out and find support. You may not know it, but you will need the support already. Many people have gone down this road, and many people will. You may be the one who brings hope—hope in the knowledge that these pets are healed and happy, and that we will all see them again.

Do My Pets Think of Me After Leaving Earth?

Since our pets are no longer limited by their physical bodies, they will think and act in different ways than on earth. But what happens in the minds of our pets after they have transitioned? Why would they choose to make us aware of their presence if they are happy and content in Paradise? In this section, we will look at more aspects surrounding our pets after they transition to the spiritual plane. If you have more questions, you will likely find the answer here.

Once your pets have entered the spiritual plane, they are not alone. They will be in the company of your loved ones that have passed. Why would this happen? You had a soul connection with your loved ones as much as you had with your pets that have crossed over. Souls in the afterlife recognize this connection and thereby find one another. It is your energy that is familiar and draws them together. Think about it this way: when a child is adopted they eventually see their adoptive parents as their own mother and father. Even though they are not the child's biological parents, the child will accept them as family. This means that they all share a connection other than blood. They share a spiritual connection that is equally strong, if not stronger sometimes.

The same rule applies to your pet. Once you have accepted a pet into your family, the pet becomes part of the family. Again, the connection is on a spiritual level. This is why the souls of those who have crossed over recognize each other, even if they had never met during their time on earth. So what happens when your pet meets their biological family in Heaven? The connection you share with your pet remains stronger, therefore, once you cross over, your pet will choose to stay with you. The spiritual connection between family, adopted or not, and between a person and their pet is unbreakable. Why? Because the connection is created through love, and love is eternal.

What happens the moment my pet leaves this world? Amazingly, according to pet psychics and animal communicators, our pets experience the same thing we do when we cross over. They become aware of their freedom and fly weightlessly into the light. They are free of sickness, pain, and suffering. The only difference between us and our pets is what happens when we get there. Adults, especially, need time to adapt to the spiritual plane. This is because our senses have been dulled by life and technology. A sudden entry into the fullness of the afterlife is a lot to bear. Therefore, adults are prepared for what lies ahead.

Animals and children share the one thing we lack as adults— pure innocence. Because they are innocent and much aware of the spiritual plane, even while in this world, they don't need to adapt. They immediately begin to play and join with other souls, familiar or unfamiliar. When adults enter Heaven, we must be prepared first. It is like taking away veil after veil, allowing us to see more with each step. Many adults who cross over experience a similar thing, according to many near-death experience statements: all the adults see something like a film playing in their heads, with them as the lead actors. They experience every important moment, good deed, but also everything wrong they did. Before the adult can continue, they must make peace with themselves first and find forgiveness. Animals and children don't need to find peace and forgiveness.

The famous psychic Matt Fraser says that after transitioning, pets go through a process where they can see everything that has happened in their lives. They see from the moment they were born, the lives they had, the moment they were adopted, and the healing changes they made to their owners' lives by choosing to love them. They also remember the pain if they were adopted and mistreated, and then the recovery after being adopted by a new loving family. They see how and why they were chosen as pets.

Pets see the beauty of the love and healing that was given to them and experience gratitude and peace. They remember how they waited for us to come home, cuddled with us, and the immense joy they felt whenever they were close to us. The process is similar to what humans experience but without guilt or a need for forgiveness. Many pets are amazed when they discover how much joy and change they brought to their owners' lives. In this regard, I especially think about therapy animals and seeing-eye dogs. Pets are also then able to learn what their purpose was when they became part of a new family. It may be that a person was going through a tough time such as illness or being bullied, and the pet arrived on time to help with healing and comfort.

There are many things that our pets don't understand while they are still in their physical bodies, such as why we take them to the veterinarian, give them pills, put ointment on wounds, have to leave them for a part of the day (such as when we go to work or go shopping), let them be groomed, refuse them certain food types, or

34

why we remove the balloon that they are about to swallow. During the *life review* process, they get to understand why all of these things happened and had to be done. This evokes a new feeling of gratitude in our pets, knowing that everything we did was because we have always loved them without condition or restriction.

Our pets do have an idea, while on earth, of when we are helping them, but also when someone is purposefully hurting them. This is why pets often behave when they visit the vet or don't hold grudges because you left them to go to work. But with the life review, our pets finally get to see what sacrifices we had to make, physically, emotionally, and financially to be able to take good care of them.

As pets are very connected to the spirit world, they mostly sense when their time to transition draws close. So, if ever you had, or have to put one of your pets to sleep, know that they know and understand that it is for their sake. They know that their time has come. People often think that in the final moments their pets are staring at them, wondering what is going on. Let me tell you, this is not the case. Your pet is staring into your eyes to let you know that everything is alright. That they understand they have to go. That stare is a *thank you* for all you have given them and been to them. They carry the thought of you from the moment of transition well into the afterlife. Your pet remembers you clearly and knows you even better than when they were with you. And they can't wait to show you their gratitude (Fraser, 2022).

Above the Pain

Now that we know our pets that have passed away live in love and harmony, free from the suffering of earth, and above all the pain, why would they come back to us? Won't they be reminded of their suffering? How will they deal with it? The moment your pet had their life review experience, they understood more about you and how much you love them. They understand pain and suffering and that it is part of the physical world. But they also understand that they are free from it, and never have to suffer again. That is *the* one message your pets that have transitioned want to bring to your attention. They don't re-live their pain when they come near to you. All they want is to be close to you, and for you to know it. When your pet transitions into the afterlife, their minds are liberated and set free from the physical world's limitations.

Some people may fear that their pet who has crossed over feels resentment. Let's look at an example: You have a pet who you love deeply, but your pet is diagnosed with a terminal illness. You try everything to prolong your pet's life. It is hard for you not to be able to be with your pet every hour of the day, because of responsibilities. There is work and family life, as well as your social life you have to focus on too. Now imagine you had to go on a business trip. It is not something you can refuse, even if you wanted to. It is an obligation you have to fulfill. Your heart aches because you have to leave your beloved pet behind.

While you are on your business trip you get a phone call—your beloved pet has passed away. Things became too complicated, and your pet had to be put to sleep. Except for your heart being torn to pieces, you also feel guilt. You weren't there when your pet needed you the most. You didn't get to spend time with your pet before they passed. What happens now? Do you feel angry, sad, and guilty all at once? It will likely be that you feel many emotions whirl through your mind and soul. You may even wonder if you will ever be able to forgive yourself for not being there. How can you ever fix this? You feel helpless, as you know you can't do anything to fix it. Or *can* you?

While you can't reverse time and steal lost moments with your pet, you don't need to feel powerless. Remember that your pet understands what you had to do and why you had to do it. They understand that you have a responsibility toward your work and that you had to go on the business trip. Your pet's mind is enlightened and opened. They won't resent you, or have you think you need their forgiveness. All your pet is feeling is love. The only pain they may feel is knowing that you are in distress. This is why they want to communicate with you. Your pet wants you to be free of pain and sorrow, just as they are.

I can tell you upfront that whenever a pet passes away or has to be put to sleep, you never need to feel guilty. Why would I say this? Pets are highly intuitive. They have abilities that surpass that of any human. I want to say that pets have psychic abilities, but that is only my opinion. Think about it—animals know when a natural disaster is about to strike, when a thunderstorm is coming, even if we have no indication of a storm yet, they know who they can trust and often are drawn to people who love animals, even when first meeting them. Our pets can sense both good and evil. They know when someone is good or bad. I'm sure we have all heard people say *I only trust people my dog trusts.* How would your dog *know* who to trust and who not to?

Where does this ability come from? It is because animals are connected to the spiritual world. Just as there are people who can predict future events in supernatural ways, so can animals. All these gifts cannot be ascribed to physical influence. What is left, then? Yes, the world beyond our own. How do guardians, guardian angels, and spirit guides know when we will need them? Because they are not limited to time and space. God, the Great Spirit, the Creator knows about future events, and as all in the spirit world share his light, love, and spirit, the knowledge is passed to them. And because our pets are connected to the spirit world, the knowledge seeps through and finds them.

Have you ever walked into a room and it felt *wrong?* This is because you became aware of its negative energy. In the same way, your pets can also sense negative energy. They are in tune with all the energies of the earth and some energies of the next world.

So, to answer the question of why you shouldn't feel guilty about your pet's passing is simply because our pets do not fear death. They understand that passing away is not the end. Yes, animals are afraid of many things; some are afraid of lightning, some of cars and buses, while some are afraid of loud noises. But death? No. The only time an animal may be afraid of passing over is if they suffer tragically before they are set free. I'm not talking about disease, but rather about matters that hurt more, such as being in an accident or being hurt otherwise, which leads to their passing.

We, as humans, fear death, because we are not as connected to the spiritual world as our pets are. Modern technology and lifestyles have robbed us of our connection to the spirit world. The light that once burned bright in us has diminished to a mere twinkle. But not for animals. Not for our pets. They are still aware, undiluted, and connected. We can learn so many things from our pets, can't we? You may wonder what would happen if we could be as intuitive as our pets. That is an excellent question and will be discussed in the next Chapter. So, stay tuned!

Have you recognized, by now, how intertwined the physical and spiritual worlds truly are? There is only a veil that separates us. As with humans, the process of transitioning from our world to the next is painless and without feelings of fear or anxiety. This is true for both animals and humans.

Perhaps you are asking what exactly our pets that have transitioned expect from us? They only want us to know that they are safe, loved, and happy. They want us to feel the same way, and not be burdened by guilt or sorrow. Grieving is necessary, but should not be forever. The only thing you should allow to be forever is love.

Happily Ever After

Larry is one of my closest friends. Like me, he is able to communicate with both people and pets that have crossed over. He doesn't like to be called a *psychic* or a *medium*. He sees himself as a vessel, simply doing the works of the Spirit. I have yet to see someone as intuitive and sensitive as he is. With sensitive, I mean attuned to the spiritual realm.

His connection with the other side is phenomenal. Larry has helped countless people to start their healing process. The fact that he is an empath makes a world of difference. He not only senses the thoughts and emotions of the living but also of those who have passed.

To be honest, there are many fake psychics out there. Many of them work by doing what we call *cold readings*. This is when the person uses psychological tricks to make people believe that they can communicate with those who have passed. Whenever you see someone for spiritual guidance and they call themselves psychic, be careful. A true communicator will be able to give you details of things that no one could even think of. Yes, the souls of those who have transitioned do not speak as we do, but rather with visions, feelings, and sometimes words. But still, a true psychic will be able to see clearly what others cannot.

There is no question that Larry is a firm believer that there are animals in the afterlife. This is not because of stories he'd read or heard or making himself guilty of reckless believing, but because of the things he has seen, heard, and experienced. Not only is he in tune with the afterlife, but has an amazing bond with animals here on earth, too. I have known Larry since we were children and since then, most of the times when we meet, he surprises or astounds me.

When we were nine years old, we walked on a dusty road on our way to his house. There were trees and bushes beside the road. Suddenly a large dog came running out of the bushes. The dog was barking loudly and aggressively. I was about to run for my life, but Larry took my hand. The dog was right behind us, barking like crazy. Larry turned around and smiled at the dog. He didn't say anything.

He just looked at the dog. I saw compassion and love stream from his eyes. The dog was silent and sat down. Larry stretched out his hand and patted the dog on his head. *He's just lonely*, Larry said softly. I looked at Larry in amazement and said, *I knew it! You are an angel!*

My peace was soon to be disrupted. I started to notice that Larry would get extremely tired very quickly. We then learned that Larry had a life-threatening condition, and he was only 12 years old. There was a hole in his heart, and he was losing a lot of blood. Tests were done and then plans were made for Larry to be operated on. In all this time I was hysterical, while Larry was calm as a breeze. He would tell me to stop worrying. Instead of me comforting him, he was the one who needed to comfort me. I felt embarrassed, angry, ashamed, and sad.

The day Larry went to the hospital to make final arrangements for his operation, he seemed different. More tests were done to determine exactly how big the hole was. Doctors came back and were speaking to his parents. It seemed like they were arguing, and Larry's parents seemed frustrated. I heard Larry's father say that he wanted a second opinion. I asked his mother what the problem was. She said: *They can't find anything wrong. They don't see any hole. It must be a mistake because there was a hole only three days ago.*

After some more tests, Larry was sent home. He was completely healed! I believed it to be a miracle. Why? Because no one deserved it more than Larry, at least that was my opinion. Later, when Larry and I were alone again, he had tears in his eyes. *I think I was in Heaven,* he said. *When?* I asked. *Last night. I could feel myself dying and leaving my body. I'm sure I was dead.* I didn't know how to react to this. Of course,

I believed him, but the thought of my best friend dying nearly made me go nuts.

I asked Larry to describe what he saw. He said that he flew up into the night sky when he saw a bright light. He flew into the light. Suddenly he was standing on a beautiful beach with silver sand. The ocean looked like molten silver, or like glass. He then saw a city that seemed to be made of pure glass-like gold. Everything was glowing. He entered the city and saw the souls of people and animals. There were the most beautiful and vibrantly colored flowers, trees, and other plants. The flowers seemed to be *alive*. All the plants were glowing too. The leaves of the trees were unlike what we have on earth. The leaves looked like emeralds gently swaying in the breezes.

The most wonderful thing to him was the music—everything was singing, the people, the plants, and the animals. But they were not singing with their mouths. He said that music was radiating from within everything and everyone, and looked like floating rainbows. He didn't hear with his ears, but as the music passed through him, he experienced the music with his soul. The music was mesmerizing and endless and could be manipulated by whoever made the music. As the light was bent, the music changed. The animals were in harmony. They all played together and were glowing with love.

The roads were also a shade of gold, glowing and translucent, with precious stones embedded in them. He was taken into what he described as a palace, with giant marble pillars laced with emeralds. He spoke to a man who said that he must return, as his work was not done. Larry cried, begging the man to let him stay. But the man told Larry that he was of better purpose in the physical world. Larry then returned and could already feel that something was different. His chest didn't hurt anymore, and he didn't get tired as easily. We believe that's when he was healed—during his visit to Heaven.

Larry said that he had learned a lot in the short time he was in Heaven. He said that, because our pets no longer have physical limitations in the afterlife, it means that we can actually *talk* to them once we get there. He also understood how loved ones and pets can visit us after they had crossed over. He explained that we, humans and animals, have a body, soul, and spirit. When we pass away, our bodies no longer hold on to our soul and spirit. Both the soul and spirit cross over. But if the person or animal wants to send their loved one a message, their souls visit earth, while their spirit remains in the afterlife. Remember, this is not a doctrine or a teaching, it is merely opinion.

It makes sense to me, as the soul contains the emotions, will, and intellect of the person or animal. The spirit is the core identity—your spirit is who you are at the deepest levels, while the same is true for your pets. So, don't worry about your pet visiting someone on earth when you cross over. You will find them there. They will meet you at the Rainbow Bridge, and you will live happily forever after.

Chapter 3

Becoming Aware

The soul itself is the center of all that we have come to call 'psychic.'
The word itself translates literally to mean "of the soul." When we
embrace our psychic potential, we embrace our soul's potential
—Kim Chestney (Sprankles, 2020)

Many people who have had near-death experiences are suddenly blessed with gifts that they didn't have before, or the gifts they already had are strengthened. Larry was no exception to this. After he visited the afterlife, Larry realized that he was even *more* in tune with souls and the world beyond the veil. This may sound wonderful, but when a gift becomes too much of a blessing, it can begin to feel like a curse. Imagine continually seeing the spirits of those who had crossed over. For Larry, it turned into a nightmare. He couldn't meet a new person without seeing a bunch of relatives who had passed away. This went on for about seven years.

He said that he had to listen to at least 30 souls talk to him at once whenever he tried to have a conversation. Spirits can be adamant, so they wouldn't allow him to have his conversation with the living person until he listened to them. Keep in mind that not all souls have urgent messages. To make things more complicated, Larry was sure that souls who had seen him in Heaven came to earth to find him. He would try and speak to someone, or do a reading when other souls come through that are not related to the person Larry was working with at all! These soul's relatives would sometimes live on the other side of the world, with no way that Larry could reach them.

To make matters even worse, many sensitives can feel and experience the way a person passed away. Larry was one of them. He felt the sensations of, for example, car accidents, being shot, being hit over the head with a sharp object, or drowning. Imagine all of these souls coming together at once and experiencing a mixed array of ways people have passed. It must be overwhelming! I wished there was something I could do to help, but my hands were tied.

He became withdrawn and didn't want to speak to anyone if he had the choice. Even when I came to visit, I could see that he was burdened. But don't worry, the story has a happy ending.

Do I Need a Medium?

You may wonder if you need a medium if you want to communicate with a loved one or a pet that has crossed over. There is no short answer to this. Let me explain by continuing with Larry's story. So, Larry was in distress. His physical, mental, and spiritual sensors were experiencing an overload. During this time, I heard some people say that they didn't understand why Larry was complaining. They would do anything to have the gift to experience the spirit world all of the time. I answered by telling them that they did not know what they were wishing for. As we are still very much part of this world, our well-being depends on our focus being on what is around us. Being constantly in touch with spirits can cause sleepless nights, feeling nauseous, anxiety, and sometimes depression.

One day when I left after visiting Larry, I was thinking about another incident that took place when we were kids. We were about 15 years old. There was a neighborhood where one of our friends, Gordon, lived that had a house with a spooky reputation. I guess every suburb has a house like this, right? Mostly everything believed about such a house is wrong, brought on by unsustained gossip and wanting the thrill of an urban legend. But the house in this neighborhood *was* scary. The owner was an old man who was seldom seen. There was a fence all around, while the bars of the gate were shaped like big diamonds.

The man who owned the house had a dog. I believe that it was a Siberian husky, as the dog was a grayish white and had the brightest blue eyes imaginable. Everyone feared the dog. The bars were shaped in such a way that this dog could put its head through one of the diamonds. For this reason, everyone avoided walking on that side of the street. As we were walking, Larry, Gordon, and I, we were getting close to the *spooky* house. Our friend said that we must cross the street as we were approaching the house. But Larry seemed like he didn't hear Gordon. He kept on walking, as if with great purpose.

When we reached the house, Gordon and I were standing in the street, begging Larry to come to us and get away from the dog. But Larry went and stood right in front of the gate, silent, looking into the yard. Suddenly the dog's head poked through a diamond and the dog grabbed Larry's hand. I nearly fainted. Larry turned to face us and smiled. *He doesn't want me to go*, Larry said. Then Larry's face changed. *This dog is hungry. His owner is not feeding him properly.* He reached into a pocket and took out some beef jerky which he gave to the dog. The dog was eating out of Larry's hand.

When we left, or actually *had* to leave, tears were coming down Larry's face. Gordon and I didn't know what to do. I asked Larry what was bothering him. Larry looked at me and said, *The dog's owner is not healthy anymore. He is unable to care for the dog. His owner is going to leave this world soon.* After that, Gordon tried to talk to his parents about it. But who would listen to teenagers? Shortly after, less than a week, Gordon phoned me and told me that the old man had passed away. When I told Larry, he cried again. I must confess, I couldn't understand why he was crying, as he didn't know the old man at all.

Larry said, *You don't know how much the dog and the old man loved each other. They were like two peas in a pod. Let's pray the dog gets a happy new home.* According to Gordon and his parents, the dog did.

After thinking about this story, I had an idea how to help Larry become focused again. I went to visit him the next day. I reminded him of his love for animals. I also reminded him that of all people, he had the highest level of inner peace I have ever witnessed. He had to get back to his passions. He had to find that peace again. I then suggested that he tried meditation and prayer, asking that his ability is limited only to those who truly needed it. I believed that the One who gave the abilities could change them too according to our needs. Why? Because we are doing good work with these abilities. They are necessary for the connection between our world and the next. We use these abilities as tools to bring hope, comfort, and to restore joy.

So, Larry followed my advice, and it worked! What I am trying to teach you through this story, is that just as Larry was able to *dim* his gifts, you are able to develop and strengthen yours. Some people don't have the means to have a pet psychic or communicator to help them. Maybe you are one of them. As we are all spiritual beings, you can learn how to connect with the spiritual realm. I'll admit, to have a pet psychic or communicator help you is never a bad idea, but that doesn't leave you without hope. Therefore, in the next sections, I will provide you with tools to become attuned to the spiritual realm and to be able to discern the presence of the soul of your beloved pet.

You can then either use this to communicate with your own pets or use your newfound talents to help others who are grieving. Once you become aware of your pet's soul, you will find that your heart starts healing, even though you once thought it impossible.

Sensitive to Their Souls

As we are still in the physical realm, you need to be able to communicate with animals in this realm first, before attempting to communicate with souls. I don't mean to scare you, but there are bad spirits out there. Many religious people (especially Christian) will tell you that communication with souls is wrong and that the souls that do communicate are evil spirits. They are only half right. Yes, evil spirits can try to communicate and pretend to be someone they are not. Evil spirits are real. You'll find them in every culture and religion across the world. The concept is not new, but ancient.

But how will you know if it is an evil spirit or truly the soul of your beloved pet? Let me answer this question in this way—imagine you have a best friend named Robert. One day your phone rings and *Robert* begins talking to you. You are used to the way he talks. He always asks kind of the same questions, has a specific nickname for you, and has a certain sense of humor. So, while you are talking to *Robert*, you realize that his voice sounds different. He calls you by your full name and not your nickname, and he lacks the humor that normally makes its appearance. What is the solution to this mystery? Yes, it is probably not Robert, but someone else pretending to be him.

If you know someone well, you'll probably realize quite quickly that the person talking to you is a different person from who they claim to be. The same is true for your pets that have passed. You know them better than anyone else. Perhaps you were not an animal communicator while they were still in our world, but still, you know them well enough to know their souls. You will recognize your pet's spirit easily. And don't fear, I will also provide you with tools and tips on how to keep yourself safe while communicating. Besides, as long as your intentions to communicate are for healing and love, there is little to no room for evil.

The Importance of Communication

Even those who are not parents understand the importance of communicating with children. From the moment a child is born, they are trying to communicate, especially needs. As they grow older, their ability to communicate improves and the parent can begin to tell what the child needs without difficulty. All of us who are pet owners will say the same thing—our pets are constantly trying to communicate. And why not? As we have determined, pets have souls, just like we do. They have thoughts, fears, feelings, personalities, and things they love. If pets know so much about themselves, wouldn't they try to communicate this to their pet-parents?

Animals, like humans, are born telepathic. Now a lot of people may go *Whoa! Telepathy? Is there really such a thing?* My answer is *yes*! It is a real thing, and we were born with it. Can this be proven? Consider this—have you ever seen a mother with a baby, where the baby can't communicate verbally at all, except for babbling? Despite this, the mother (or father) knows what the baby wants. For example, the baby may be babbling, when their mother says something like, *Oh, she just wants her pacifier.* When it is given to the baby, the baby is quiet and happy. The point is, how do the parents know what the baby wants? It's no coincidence, it's telepathy.

Other examples are when you hear your phone ringing, and you know who it is that is calling, even when you haven't seen their name on your phone or answered yet. Or you hear the doorbell ring (when you don't have plans for any visitors), and you know who is at your gate? Telepathy is not limited to empaths or sensitives but is an ability

51

all of us share. The reason it is not strong in many people is that we have suppressed this talent with technology and modern beliefs. But, time and again, it rears its little head. The first thing you need to do is to reactivate your telepathic ability. Animals do not communicate with words, but with thoughts and feelings. Therefore, telepathy is vital to understanding your pets.

Understand that animals see who you are to the core. They know your soul and your spirit. They recognize the vibrations of energy that reside in you. Your pets also hear you, not only physically, but also what is in your soul. They react to your tone, intent, and attitude. Now all you need to do is learn how to listen to your pets. What do you experience when you are petting or stroking your pets? It feels good, doesn't it? Not only is this the equivalent of grooming your pet, but your pet also feels your vibrations, energy, and what you are feeling in your heart. This is healing to both yourself and your pets. This is also why your pets know when you are feeling down or upset. They act differently around you because they know something is wrong. Most pets will try to comfort you. They understand pain, I believe, more than we give them credit for.

How do you talk to your pet? If you have something important to say, first think about what you are going to say. Create a clear picture of it in your mind. What is it you want to tell your pet, and why is it so important? Then, practice what you want to tell your pet. Say it out loud. Are your emotions and thoughts on the same frequency as the message? Will your pet experience the right energy associated with the message? Are you able to clearly visualize the message you want to give your pet? Keep on practicing until you feel that your heart and mind are in sync. Next, talk to your pet. Remember to focus not only on the message, but also on the intent, attitude, and energy you are using to convey the message. Make sure that you have your pet's full attention.

After you have done this, pay attention to your pet. Are they behaving differently? Does it seem like your message had an impact? If it was a behavior that needed to be corrected, did it work? Giving your pet a deeper message may take some time to achieve, but keep on practicing. The exercise of practicing alone already strengthens the spiritual connection between you and your pet.

Whispers in the Storm

Now that you have learned about the foundation of animal communication, we can move on to communicating with pets that have crossed over. Your pets that have transitioned would love to communicate with you. In this session, you will learn how to reignite your abilities.

Calming Your Mind

The world we live in is very demanding, which can leave us feeling drained, unfocused, and anxious. As it is important to be filled with positive energy while maintaining a calm mind while communicating, you have to calm your mind before starting. We cannot do anything to change the world or our responsibilities, which means we have to change what is happening within us, in our minds. To calm your mind, you have to narrow down everything you are focusing on until it becomes one thing, which is the present moment. You can find music for meditation that you can play in the background while doing this exercise.

Take deep breaths. Feel how the air moves into your body, and out again as you exhale. Focus on your breathing. If your mind wanders, that's okay. Just be patient and bring it back to your breathing. Keep on doing this until you are fully focused on your breathing. Be completely aware of every sensation that comes with breathing, what it feels like when you inhale and when you exhale.

Feel your mind resting and creating space. Be aware of the fact that you are in control of your focus. Keep on taking deep breaths. Breathe in, and breathe out. Imagine yourself floating above a desert. You see the beautiful patterns in the sand, passing over dunes in a cool breeze. Still keep on focusing on your breathing. Feel how this focus overflows into the rest of your body. Your body is becoming aware of your intent and enters a complete state of relaxation. Decide that while you are communicating, you will take one step at a time while maintaining your calm and peaceful mindset. You won't allow yourself to be rushed. You will remain in control and focused.

Protecting Yourself

Make sure that you are comfortable before you start. It should be a room without technology, such as a television set, radio, or even your cell phone. You must make every effort to ensure that you won't be distracted, as you need to remain calm, clear-minded, and focused throughout the process. For the same reason, surround yourself with neutral colors and remove any objects that may distract you.

I recommend that you don't try to communicate while you are upset or in a bad mood. Energy has a direct influence on the souls and spirits you will attract. The energy needs to be pure, positive, and filled with love, therefore, establish your intent before you start. Think of the pet you want to communicate with. You may look at photos and videos of the pet, remembering how much you love them. Feel this love flow through you and radiate from you. Spirits are drawn to energy, so it is a good idea to light some white candles. White symbolizes purity, peace, and harmony. You can light a blue candle as well, which will represent Heaven and the afterlife.

If you want, you can smudge the room by using sage. This will purify the room of any lingering negative energy. You can use crystals too. Crystals are scientifically proven to vibrate at different frequencies (American Institute of Physics, 2018). You can place a rose quartz crystal to generate loving energy, and rhodonite to enhance the healing of emotional wounds.

Do a prayer in which you ask God or your guides to protect you from harm. Don't be nervous while trying to communicate. Let the communication happen naturally and in a calm manner. If you find that you are becoming nervous, picture a stream of murky water. See the murky water being washed away and becoming all the more clear until you can see the pebbles on the bottom. This symbolizes your mind and how it is being cleansed from negative thoughts and feelings.

While you are communicating, remember to be courteous. Speak to the souls like you would want others to speak to you—with dignity and respect. Use words such as *please* and *thank you*. Once you are done communicating, end your session by saying: *I close the door that I have opened.* Visualize a door closing, which is the door to the other side. If you are starting to feel overwhelmingly uneasy, rather end your session immediately. When you fill your heart and the room you are using with positivity and love, chances are minimal that anything else will try to communicate but your loving pet.

Communication may not work the first time you try it. Keep on practicing by trying and trying again. You also don't need to do it alone. If there is another person who is open-minded and willing to be with you, allow them. Your pet won't mind.

Clairvoyance

Many people think that clairvoyance is a gift only destined for some, while others see it as a big taboo. The fact is that we are all born with telepathy, clairvoyance, clairaudience, clairsentience, and claircognizance. How do I know that? These abilities are linked directly with the spirit world, and we all have a body, spirit, and soul. Because your soul and spirit will continue to exist while your body will not, your soul and spirit are eternal. Therefore, they must have ways to communicate. We won't only have a spirit once we cross over, we have it all our lives. This means that our spiritual abilities are present, whether we are aware of them or not.

Have you ever seen something moving from the corner of your eye and when you look, there's nothing there? Or have you ever looked at a person or a pet intently and then seen a color surrounding them? It is like a colored bright haze that appears to outline them. To test this, let someone place their hand against a white wall in a brightly lit room. Stare at their hand intently. You will begin to see a colored outline, sometimes thick, sometimes thinner. It is not a trick your eyes play on you. What you are seeing is their aura or spirit energy.

Clairvoyance is the ability to see things, people, or events that cannot be seen naturally with the naked eye in a supernatural way. While some people's clairvoyant abilities are stronger, we all have the skill, strong enough to make contact with those who have passed. Being clairvoyant doesn't mean that you will start seeing things physically. It is a spiritual experience. For example, when your mind is calm and focused, you may receive an image from the spirit world. It will not be something you are thinking about. You will immediately know that it is not your own thoughts, but ones that have been sent to you.

Receiving such images or messages depends on your clairvoyant ability. Did you know that your intuition and clairvoyant abilities are directly linked to your pineal gland? Your pineal gland is situated between your eyes and is often referred to as the *third eye*. It is only called this, as your pineal gland also has the ability to see things. This gland is your brain's direct connection to the spiritual realm. In studies done on habit formation, it was found that your brain creates neural pathways whenever you perform a new action. But that's not all. Your brain also creates neural pathways when you imagine or visualize something.

Let's test this, shall we? Imagine yourself on a beautiful white-sand beach. You can see the blue ocean and hear the waves coming in and crashing on the shore. You feel the cool sea breeze around you. Sit back, close your eyes, and imagine this for a while. What happens to your mind? You begin to feel different, don't you? It is like your body is responding as if you really are there. This is why motivational speakers often tell people to imagine themselves being successful, happy, or healthy. They also tell people to imagine themselves being able to do something that seems difficult and imagining themselves achieving their goals. The process of visualization creates a neural network that aids you in doing what needs to be done, as your brain now believes that you can do it.

What does this have to do with clairvoyance? I am about to give you some practical exercises to enhance your clairvoyant ability. These exercises require imagination and visualization. Now that you understand the power of visualization, you know that these exercises will indeed be effective.

Just like any other muscle in your body, your brain can exercise. To increase the strength of your brain and pineal gland, play memory games. I recommend playing the memory card game, where all the cards are placed upside down and you have to find matches. But this time while you are playing it, try to visualize the cards with your mind's eye and see how accurate you are. The more you do it, the more you exercise your pineal gland. You'll soon be surprised at how you know which cards are matches, with less effort. At first, you may not be able to *see* what the cards are, but that's no problem. Be kind and patient with yourself, always.

For the next exercise, you'll be laying down on your bed. Be as comfortable as possible. Place a small quartz crystal on your forehead, between your eyes, right on your pineal gland. Close your eyes, and imagine that there is a crystal ball inside of your head. Now picture yourself lighting a candle in the center of the crystal ball. Please don't light a physical candle on your head! You're only imagining it.

Next, visualize the light within the crystal ball becoming brighter with each breath you take, until it is filled with bright light. Now imagine a bright tunnel that starts at your pineal gland and runs right through to the back of your head. Also imagine a bright tunnel that starts at the top of your head and ends at your root chakra, which is at the base of your spine. Picture these two bright tunnels as forming a type of cross within your body. Visualize this cross pulsing with bright light. Imagine your mind's eye opening, allowing you to see the spiritual realm clearly.

The more you do this exercise, the more neural pathways you build in your brain to empower the pineal gland. In turn, the energy associated with your intention will focus on opening your mind's eye, strengthening your clairvoyant ability.

To help you focus on your intent, you can do the next exercise. You can sit upright for this exercise. Visualize yourself holding seven balloons, each a different color of the rainbow. Picture yourself being outside if you are indoors. Imagine that you are letting go of the red balloon. Watch it, in your mind's eye, as it slowly floats further and further up into the sky until it disappears. Repeat this visualization with the other colors; orange, yellow, green, blue, indigo and violet.

The next exercise is focused on your aura. Make sure that the room is not too bright. A dimly lit room works best when you try to see your own aura. Set your intention that you are going to see your aura, believing that you will. With your fingers making loose fists, bring your hands together, but don't let them touch. Extend the index finger of both hands, allowing them to touch. Rub your index fingers together for between three to five minutes. You can change the position of your hands, as long as your index fingers keep touching and rubbing against each other. Slowly pull them apart, only a tiny distance. Look at the area between your fingers. Focus, and you should be able to see a colorful mist-like light between them. This is your aura or energy field. Exciting, isn't it? If you don't see your aura at first, keep on doing this exercise. You will see your aura soon enough.

Clairaudience

Clairaudience is when you *hear* a message, but cannot identify a physical source. It is about hearing a voice speak to you, not into your ears, but straight into your mind. Some people have such experiences but don't realize it. For example, when you clearly hear someone calling your name, but either no one did, or it happens while you are all alone. Messages may sometimes be mistaken for your own thoughts, but the important part is to interpret and understand the message. In this way, you will be able to determine whether it was your inner voice or came from the spiritual realm.

Let's work on strengthening your clairaudient ability. Use the exercise of the murky stream, visualizing it becoming clearer, as a way to calm your mind and gain focus. Close your eyes, and ask for a phrase to be placed in your mind. You can say something like *Pure loving souls, please place one word in my mind.* Relax while taking deep breaths to allow the word to appear in your consciousness. Remain calm and wait patiently to receive it. In this exercise, don't overanalyze or worry that you have placed a word in your own mind. Once you have received a word, write it down.

Close your eyes, relax, and clear your mind by taking a few deep breaths. Now say: *Pure loving souls, please place two words in my mind.* Stay relaxed, take deep breaths, and wait patiently for the two words. The words you receive may seem strange, but don't think about it for now. Just write the words down. Keep in mind that people don't receive messages in the same way. Words may be given to you in a whisper, a thought that appears, or a clear audible voice. Your thoughts should be constrained, as they can be counterproductive during this process. Go about this exercise with child-like faith and trust. Your brain is not at work during this practice, it is a completely spiritual experience.

Let's try the exercise once more. Close your eyes and take deep breaths to clear your mind. Say: *Pure loving souls, please place a phrase in my mind.* Remain calm and relaxed while taking deep breaths. Wait patiently for the phrase to be given. Once you have received the phrase, write it down. When you are done with the exercise, look at what you have written, determining the message that was given to you. In the context of this book, you may have set your intent on hearing from your pet that has crossed over. Considering that, does the meaning of the words you have written change? What is your beloved pet trying to communicate? If you struggle to connect the dots, repeat the exercise and request more phrases from your pet.

Clairsentience

In simple terms, clairsentience means that you feel emotions associated with people or events. Larry is clairsentient, as he can feel the emotions of people and animals both of this world and the next, as well as the intensity of the event in which they passed.

Don't worry, not a lot of people have the ability to that extreme. Clairsentience is vital in communicating with your pet who has crossed over, as animals communicate especially with emotions. It may be that you already have a level of clairsentience. Let's do a test to determine the level you're at.

⊙ Do you have amazing intuition, often knowing of events that are taking place even when you are not present, have knowledge of past events when you have never heard or seen anything about it, or similarly even future events? Do you often know, just by meeting someone, whether you can trust them? Do you often know when something is a bad idea, even when everyone else thinks it's not?

⊙ Do people label you as overly sensitive or accuse you of being too emotional? Do you often see hidden intent, whether good or bad, which can cause your emotions to stir? Do you become very emotional when you are watching videos about heart-touching stuff, or when you see someone crying, even strangers?

⊙ Have you ever felt uncomfortable or physically ill with no explanation, only to find out that the place that you visited was filled with negative energy?

- ⊙ Do you become anxious sometimes while you are handling antiques?

- ⊙ Do you dislike going to places such as shopping malls, as you feel overwhelmed when there are a lot of people around you?

- ⊙ Do you often know what people or animals are feeling, even understanding and recognizing hidden emotions?

- ⊙ Can you easily *read between the lines*, understanding hidden jokes or comments even when others don't catch the true meaning?

- ⊙ Do people often come to you for advice or with secrets, as you are seen as an excellent listener?

- ⊙ Do you like to use phrases such as *I sense that…* or *I feel…*?

- ⊙ Do you often feel chills or get goosebumps for no apparent reason?

If you have answered *yes* to all or some of these questions, you have the gift of clairsentience. Well, everyone has the gift, but your answers determine whether yours is active. It may be that you have been labeled as *overly emotional*, but don't worry, it simply means that your level of clairsentience is higher than that of your accusers.

As with the other abilities, clairsentience can be exercised too. The best way is by developing a relationship with your intuition. Every time your intuition tells you something, write it down. Whenever the truth comes out about your hunches, compare it to what you have written down. In this way, you can determine how accurate your intuition is. To cleanse your intuitive energies and recharge, spend time in nature. Take off your shoes and feel your energy flow to the earth and the earth's energy to you.

Claircognizance

Claircognizance is about supernaturally gaining knowledge. Just to be clear, some people immediately think of things such as black magic and evil witches when they hear the word *supernatural*. But supernatural is simply a term used for everything that is not subject to the laws of nature or science. In other words, everything people can't explain. When you ask people to explain the spiritual realm, spirits, or souls, no one will be able to give you a clear answer. Why? Because the spirit world is part of the supernatural, something that defies the laws of nature and science. But does this make the supernatural any less real? No, the term was coined as such things do exist, without a doubt.

Back to the subject of claircognizance. Have you ever had knowledge about people, objects, animals, or events that you shouldn't know of? I'm not talking about taking an informative or good guess, I'm talking about knowing something beyond doubt. Do people often ask you *How did you know?* This may mean that you already are claircognizant. Let's look at ways you can exercise this ability.

Meditate as often as you can, preferably daily. You can listen to soft music for meditation or sit in silence. Focus a lot on your breathing and feel the air coming into your body and leaving as you exhale. Practice different feelings and moods. Imagine during one session that you are on a beach, for the next session, picture yourself in a beautiful, lush forest, and for the next, imagine being on top of a mountain with the world spread out far and wide. You can think of your own scenarios. If you need to clear your mind, use the cleansing-of-the-stream method. Go out at night during a full moon, and let the moonlight wash over you. Feel yourself being filled with energy and light.

You may also want to sit quietly, imagining a vortex appearing above you. Picture the vortex growing until it surrounds you. Another method of exercise is practicing automated writing. Take a pen and a piece of paper, and start writing without thinking about what you are writing. Keep on saying things like *I am waiting for something to write. Guides, beloved souls, I am waiting patiently for you to give me something to write.* Afterward, look at what you have written. Can you make out words or phrases? Some of it may be knowledge that came to you from the spirit world.

In a nutshell, clairvoyance is what you see spiritually, clairaudience is what you hear in the spirit, clairsentience is what your spirit feels, and claircognizance is what your spirit knows. There you have it. It's time to get supernatural!

Chapter 4

Hidden in Plain Sight

If you accept that pets can love us as much as we do them, then the logic is clear and cannot be denied. If you believe that there is a heaven for people, then they must be there, waiting for us, when we cross over. Heaven is love, and pets always share that with us
—Wallace Sife (Ingram, 2020).

Imagine that you have transitioned to the afterlife. The sights are amazing, and you feel love and peace in abundance. Does this mean that you will forget your loved ones who are still on the physical plane? Or would you want them to know that you are loved and at peace? You would likely want to let them know that you still love and think of them. How would you do this? You will try sending messages through dreams, signs, symbols, or if they are sensitive enough, communicate through their clairvoyance.

Your pets are the same. They haven't forgotten you and are aware of your grief. They want to communicate their love and the fact that love is forever. Similar to what you would do, they are sending messages. The only problem is, we don't always know where to look and how to see these messages.

Interpretations in Recorded History

The rulers of ancient times relied heavily on signs and symbols to ensure that they are on the right track. People in ancient Mesopotamia started recognizing signs and symbols as messages as early as 3,000BC. However, the first interpretations must have been vocalized instead of written down, as the first written interpretations are only found 1,000 years after writing was invented. In ancient times these signs and symbols were not used for personal healing or conveying messages of love, but mostly for divination. People in Mesopotamia and Babylon believed that the messages came from gods and ancestors. In ancient Mesopotamia, for example, signs were interpreted as a message foretelling a king's death, whereafter rituals were performed to prevent the king from dying. Therefore, they didn't see the message as the cause of harm, but rather a warning.

Babylonian and Mesopotamian interpretations were recorded and started to spread to other cultures, such as Jewish, Assyrian, Aramaic, Chinese, and Greek. In the Mandaean culture, messages were read from the way a crow caws, a fire crackles, clouds are shaped, a door creaks, and the color of dust clouds. Many cultures started creating their own ways of receiving messages, such as pouring oil, throwing marked stones, or interpreting the movement of smoke.

In ancient Babylon, interpretations were often accompanied by moral lessons, many of which turned into fables. These fables often had animals as the main characters. It is clear then that ancient people had a great reverence for animals. Almost everything was interpreted as a sign, message, or omen. They carefully observed the sun, moon, stars, and planets and waited for the gods to give them celestial signs. But they also found messages in the way the wind blew, feathers, animal behavior, the formation in which birds were flocking, clouds, and more. But, who knows, maybe they truly were able to interpret messages in all these things. After all, they were very intuitive and focused on the spiritual realm (Annus, 2010).

Glimpses in Unexpected Places

Although your pets that have transitioned will communicate on a spiritual level, it will likely also happen that they give you physical signs and symbols. People often write these messages off as coincidence, but what if what they saw or heard was no coincidence, but a message their beloved pet wished for them to receive. Therefore, you should also be aware of how to physically look for signs, symbols, and signals.

In this section, we'll be looking at physical signs that your pet may be trying to communicate. These instances are based on people's testimonies, who believed that their pets who have passed tried to make their presence known. Perhaps you will recognize some of these signs. Your pets will try to communicate immediately after their passing and keep doing so for years to come. Remember that your pets that have transitioned are no longer bound to a physical body. Time is of no relevance to them and their love and memories of you will never fade.

Also, keep in mind that pets won't try to communicate as a novelty or simply *because they can*. They want to convey a message. It may be that they know you are grieving or upset, want you to know that they still love you and think of you, or are trying to bring healing and light into your life. When you become aware of the signs they may be using to communicate, consider how you feel when you notice them. Though the sign may be physical, its impact will influence your mind, body, and spirit.

Believing is Seeing

Sometimes when you least expect it, you may see your pet for a split second. Many people think that this is their imagination, but what if you weren't specifically thinking about your pet at that moment? These unexpected glimpses are not coincidental or due to imagination. It takes a lot of energy for a spirit to manifest, which means that your pets can only make themselves visible for a split second. Other things you may see include objects being moved, even slightly, shapes in the clouds that look like your pet, or it may be hair, feathers, or other items that can be associated with your pet appearing in your house.

It may also happen that your gaze is drawn at the clock at certain times. If this is the same time every day or regularly, what is the significance of the time? Take some time to think about it. Was it the time you met your pet, when your pet passed away, or when you liked to spend a lot of time with your pet? You may also consider that the time may actually be referring to a date. For example, you may be drawn to the clock at 15:11. This can refer to a date, which means the 15th of November may be of importance.

Some people, especially cat owners, claimed that they would see new scratch marks appear, even though their only cat has passed away. There may be a smudge on a glass door or window indicating a pet's nose pressed up against it. You may also see unexplainable markings or footprints left by your pet. When you find feathers in unusual places, your pet is likely trying to give you a sign. Your attention may also be drawn to the television, newspaper, a billboard, or anywhere that you can read something, and you'll see your pet's name on there.

You may find unusual objects around the house with no explanation of where they come from. Do you have light bulbs that continue to go out? When did it start? Was it shortly after your pet had passed away? Spirits can influence electricity, so if your light bulbs or any electrical appliances are going wonky, it may be caused by the presence of your pet's spirit. It may also happen that your heart stops for a moment when you see something like a towel on the ground because for a moment it looked like your pet. It may have been the spirit of your pet using the object to draw your attention. Although it turns out only to be a towel, you may have actually sensed your pet's presence.

Observe the behavior of your other pets if you have any. As pets are sensitive to the spiritual realm, they may be aware of your pet visiting from the afterlife. If your pets are reacting to something you can't see, it may be a sign that your beloved pet is with you. Your other pets may also behave similarly as they would have when your pet was still in the physical world. For example, when playing, one pet may have jumped around happily. If your pet is alone and jumping around, they may be playing with their pet-sibling's soul. It may take a while for the pets that are still physically with you to adapt to the spirit of their sibling, but once they have, they'll share many more moments together.

Have you ever visited family or friends who have pets, and then for a moment, their pet had the same look in their eyes as you saw in your pet? Perhaps the way they pull their face, or how they come to sit on your lap is similar to what your pet always did. It's no coincidence—it is your pet trying to communicate. Let's say, for example, you had a white cat with black spots. You may see a white butterfly with black spots on its wings in unusual places. If your attention is strangely drawn to it, it is likely your pet's doing.

Basically, look for anything strange or out of place. It may be a dent in your pillow, proof of something that had moved on your bed, kitchen cupboards opening, unexplainable puddles of water, or muddy footprints.

Dreaming About Your Pets

You may be dreaming about your pet that has passed. The dream can include your pets that are still in the physical world too. If these are pets that you got after your pet has passed away, it may be that your pet wants you to know that they are happy you found joy in your new pets. Some people find it hard to move on and adopt a new pet, as they fear they may be dishonoring the memory of their pet who has transitioned. In such a case, or whenever you are feeling down or sad, your pet may appear to you in dreams to bring you love and comfort. Also, remember that your pets that have transitioned are not jealous.

They are bathed in so much love and light, and that is all there is. There is no jealousy or resentment.

Dreams are not only meant for us to deal with psychological issues. The spirit world knows how to use dreams to communicate. People have known this since ancient times. Scientists can't fully explain what dreams are, let alone what dreams may be used for. The most important thing is to keep loving. One way to keep the love going is to pass it on to new pets. There is no need to be anxious or fearful. Your pet knows that you love them. They know that this love is eternal. Therefore, they want to see you happy and smiling. They love you as much as you love them.

Bursts of Happy Memories

How often does it happen that you unexpectedly think of a happy moment you shared with your pet? Do these memories make you smile? When you are not actively thinking about your pet and happy memories pop up suddenly, it may be the spirit of your beloved animal placing those memories in your mind. In this way they can communicate their love, how grateful they are for the time you had together on earth, or just to let you know that they are alright and thinking about you. Some people see this as a normal psychological reaction, but a reaction to what? Thoughts don't just fall out of nowhere. They are either placed there by yourself, or someone else.

What Was That Sound?

Many people claimed to have received audible cues from their pets who have crossed over. Should you hear something you can't easily explain, these sounds are meant to serve as messages, meaning that your pet wants you to know that they are near. Let's look at some sounds that your pet may be using to draw your attention.

- ⊙ You may hear scratching, such as when your pet wanted to tell you to let them out of or into the house. Or it may be that you had a cat and can hear sounds like a cat sharpening their claws. You may also hear nails tapping on the floor as if your pet is still running around.

- ⊙ There may be thuds or bumps you hear, such as when a pet jumped on a counter or table, or a sound similar to when your pet wagged their tail and it thudded against furniture.

- ⊙ When you hear faint barking that you can't explain, it may be your pet. Sometimes the barking sounds close but muffled. There may be sounds of other pets, such as a bird chirping or singing or the meowing of a cat.

- ⊙ Did your pet wear a collar with a small bell? You may sometimes hear a bell jingling unexpectedly. That would be your pet making their presence known.

- ⊙ If you have or had a doggy door, you may hear it flapping.

- ⊙ You may even hear floors creaking or clear animal-like footsteps.

- ⊙ If your pet had a favorite toy, you may hear inexplicable sounds that would have come from that specific toy.

It may also happen that your attention is drawn to a song playing on the radio or television. Was this a song you sang to your pet, or maybe it's a song that reminds you of your time together? If so, it is likely your pet telling you that they are missing you too.

Fuzzy Feelings

Did you know that you can sometimes feel your pet that has transitioned? It may be direct or indirect. The more direct sensations would be feeling like a pet is rubbing up against your leg, touching your shoulder, or trying to touch you in any way they can. Indirect sensations can include laying in bed and it feels like something just jumped on the bed with you, but with nothing in sight. It may also happen while you're on the couch, or anywhere for that matter. Your pet is no longer limited to time and space—they can make their presence known whenever and wherever they feel they have to.

If you notice spots with higher temperatures, it may be your pet's spirit being present. This is especially true if the temperature spot is where your pet used to sleep or love to spend time. If you are laying in bed or sitting on the couch and you feel warmth next to you, it is probably your pet spending some time with their beloved pet-parent.

Follow Your Nose

Every pet has their own unique smell. Some are a bit more pleasant than others, but still. It may happen that your nose catches a whiff of something familiar unexpectedly, and when you think about it, the smell once belonged to your beloved pet. Or perhaps your pet loved a certain snack with a distinct smell. Whenever you smell this snack it is your pet trying to communicate. If there was a favorite type of shampoo you used for your pet, you may smell that too. You may even smell your pet's breath, or when it rains, smell wet fur.

Isn't it wonderful to know that your beloved pets that have transitioned still want to be with you and want you to know that they are near? I think it is truly amazing and proof of eternal love. You may have had pets as a child many, many years ago. Those pets are still thinking about you and may be giving you signs daily. Keep your senses sharp and be aware of your surroundings. Signs from your beloved pets may be subtle, so be aware.

Finding Assurance

We know now that pets are very psychic and connected to the spirit world. They know, for example, when a storm is coming, a natural disaster is about to strike, or if someone is a good or bad person. How often have you heard of a pet dog, or other animals, that attacked intruders? With so many people coming into your home, how does your pet know who to allow and who they should attack? It happens because they can sense a person's soul and intent. What's more amazing is that it may take time for us to know a person's intentions or whether they are *good or bad*, yet a pet can tell instantly. Wow! What an amazing ability! Therefore, there is no doubt left that your pets have always been psychic—they can and want to communicate with you from the spiritual realm.

While in nature, you find animals that warn people of pending danger. Many animals are spiritually inclined to help us and it doesn't end when they pass away. Your pets are still around, doing their best to protect you from harm. Have you ever met a person and heard growling that you can't explain? It may have been your pet trying to warn you. The greater the love, the stronger the bond. This also means that while your pet was still in the physical world, their intuition and sixth sense helped to strengthen the bond you share. We connect directly with the souls of our pets and they connect directly with ours.

The thing I look forward to most is meeting my pets at the Rainbow Bridge and having them accompany me as I walk through the gates to the afterlife. We will not be separated from them, but spend eternity together. It is good to know that our pets aren't alone. Not only are they with other pets, playing together and enjoying themselves, but they are also with our loved ones who have already crossed over. Why does this happen? When you adopt a pet, they become part of your family. It is recognized here on earth and also in the afterlife.

Here's something that may be surprising—people who have passed come to visit their pets too. For example, your grandfather had a little dog who loved sleeping on his lap. But your grandfather's time had come to transition to the spiritual realm. Let's call the little dog *Rex*. Rex ends up living with you. You may notice strange behaviors from the dog sometimes, as he is running up and down, playing with someone you don't see. You wouldn't need to worry, as it is just your grandfather coming to visit his favorite pup. This means that the pet still is important, just as much as when their owner was still in this world. What a powerful connection!

Some people believe that many pets are divinely appointed to their forever homes. I tend to believe that too. This may be the perfect reason why many people connect with their pets immediately, even only after meeting them. I have often heard people say things like *from the first moment I met my pet, I fell in love*. It is most likely that the pet felt the same way. How else can we explain such a deep, instant, yet durable connection? It may also be that you had pets that should have been temporary, with your house serving as a foster home, but you became so attached that you adopted these pets yourself. How else can this happen if it was not meant to be? Perhaps God, the Universe, the Great Spirit, or whatever deity you believe in knew that you and this pet need each other and that you will love each other forever.

It may also happen that your pet guides you to an animal that needs the love and support only you can give. Most of the time you won't be aware that it was your pet's doing. Your pet knows your soul and now that they have crossed over, know and understand you even better. Yes, nothing can take the place of a beloved pet and you never need to stop loving them, still, you have physical love and care available to give a pet here on earth. Meeting new pets who need loving homes won't dishonor the memory of your beloved pet. Rather, it will honor them. Your pet will look on happily and proudly to see you moving forward and pouring your love onto another pet who needs it so terribly.

If you have recently lost a pet, or know of someone who did, let's talk about how you can get through it. The loss of a pet is always traumatic, no one can tell you otherwise. Anyone who is an animal lover knows that it is devastating when a pet passes away. People who are not pet-parents don't know that it feels the same as when a parent loses a child. You feel helpless, emotional, and crushed. Some people have guilt and self-resentment. Others may feel anger or like they are going to drown in agony.

First of all, understand that grieving is a normal process. No amount of good news or promises can take the pain away. Yes, you know that your pet is waiting for you at the Rainbow Bridge, but their spot here in the physical world is empty. You can't hold them or touch them like you used to. Grief is experiencing the loss of a loved one, or in this case, a beloved pet. Determine all of the feelings you have. Write these feelings down. Do you feel things such as sadness, loneliness, guilt, or remorse? It may sound like a horrible suggestion, but hold on—there's a good reason behind this.

Feelings of guilt make you beat yourself up and can be destructive to your soul. Consider what you would have done if roles were reversed. Would you want the ones in the physical realm to punish themselves? You wouldn't. You'd want them to be happy and reassure them of your love. That's all your pets want to do while waiting for you at the Rainbow Bridge. They want you to heal, love, and find your joy again. Just as you would, they will do anything to make your heart whole again. Imagine that you can put all of the love you have for your pet that has crossed over in a big basket. Will you put it away in a dark, cold storeroom, or will you present it to another pet who needs this kind of love and care? You love your pets, therefore you do your best. Your pet knows this. Remember that always.

Chapter 5

Will My Pet Come Back to Me?

I am confident that there truly is such a thing as living again,
that the living spring from the dead, and that the souls of
the dead are in existence
—Socrates (Das, 2019).

The concept of reincarnation is believed by many people, even those of high esteem. What is your belief regarding reincarnation? Some will try to fight the thought, yet there are many believers and also people who are certain that they experienced proof of reincarnation, whether it is a loved one or a beloved pet. In this chapter, we will delve deep into the concept of reincarnation and see why your pet will likely choose to come back to you.

From a Global Perspective

Every religion and culture in the world has a concept of the afterlife. Though there are differences, many of these religions agree on the subject of reincarnation. Some of these religions believe in the reincarnation of both humans and animals. Reincarnation is defined as the rebirth of a soul into a new physical body. This means that religions agree that every living being is body, soul, and spirit (although in some religions the soul and spirit are combined) and that the body only serves as a vessel while the soul and spirit are eternal.

The Peyote Way

Native Americans revere nature and have the utmost respect for all animals. They believe that all spirits are one with the universe and therefore take part in the cycle of reincarnation, animals, humans, and even plants. Animals and plants reincarnate to inhabit a body in the same region where they lived previously. Because of their belief, namely that animals, humans, plants, insects, and objects have spirits, they value conservation and protection of nature. It is also the belief that some humans can allow their souls to leave their bodies and inhabit animals or other objects for periods of time. Inuit and Native American people speak about animals with the same respect as they do humans. Animals are important to the extent that totems are created in the image of animals, which they believe are their protectors.

As they believe that everything has a spirit, they do not see man as the master of creation or the universe, but rather as merely a part of it. Not only do they believe in reincarnation, but also that the souls of humans and animals can serve as helping spirits or guardians. These spirits are mainly of relatives who guide humans when they need wisdom or direction. This means that every animal and human, whether they are still in the physical world or have crossed over, have a purpose to fulfill.

Buddhism

The transference of energy is important in Buddhism. The Buddhist idea of karma is the ever-changing state of a person, because of moral energy that is emitted and received. The energy the person receives is based on their actions. Therefore, karma is not fate and can be controlled. Reincarnation is a process that ends when the soul has reached enlightenment and no longer has earthly desires. The manner a soul reincarnates depends on their karma. The belief is that the soul can be reincarnated into one of six realms. There are three heavenly and three hellish realms. To be reincarnated as a human falls under a heavenly realm, while rebirth as an animal is considered a hellish realm.

It sounds terrible, but what it means is that the soul that is reborn as an animal needs help and guidance. Therefore, those who practice Buddhism must always help animals and be kind to them. Being good toward an animal helps with karmic energy and will improve the person's chance to be reincarnated into a heavenly realm, or to achieve enlightenment. Therefore, they believe that their pets have souls and include their pets in their religious practices, such as chants, worship, or meditation.

Mormons

Although Mormons do not believe in reincarnation itself, they do believe that the spirits of animals, plants, and humans existed before they came into the physical plane. This means that they also believe that spirits are eternal and that there is an afterlife for all.

Islam

In the old Islamic tradition, animals were considered as not to have souls. However, this view has changed in modern times. Many now believe that animals have souls too and will be part of the cycle of reincarnation. They believe, however, that reincarnation has nothing to do with reward or punishment, but is rather a process of spiritual evolution. This view has changed since many acknowledge the worldwide scientific status of reincarnation. They believe that animal souls are eternal. Although they believe that humans and animals will be judged eventually, animals will not be judged the same way as humans.

Sikhism

In Sikhism, the belief is that all souls are reincarnated, animals and humans. In many other cultures, the souls that inhabit animals may one day progress to the point where the soul can inhabit a human body. This is not the case in Sikhism—they believe that only humans can achieve the highest level of spirituality to become one with God. The souls of animals cannot *become* human. But that, I must admit, is good enough for me. I'd love to spend eternity playing with my furry pet-children!

Still, because those who practice Sikhism believe that animals have souls, all animals must be treated with kindness and be taken care of.

Hinduism

Hinduism offers a lot to teach, as it is one of the oldest religions on earth. They believe that humans and animals take part in the cycle of reincarnation. They believe that humans can be reincarnated as animals, depending on the person's deeds. This is also a karmic belief where a person has to *deserve* to be reborn as a human being. Although being born as an animal is a punishment for their bad deeds, it is crucial in Hinduism that all animals must be treated with kindness and respect, and must be cared for.

The mistreatment of animals is deeply frowned upon as they believe it can alter your karmic state for the worst. Animals do not enjoy the same state of liberty and freedom as humans, therefore it is up to humans to protect and guide them. This means that all animals receive wonderful treatment from humans. Animal rights advocates love the Hindu point of view regarding the treatment of animals. Their belief is that all beings, humans, and animals, are manifestations of Brahman, and from this point of view all living things deserve equal respect.

Although there are different beliefs, two things catch the attention—there *is* an afterlife and animals *do* have souls. If so many religions believe that both animals and humans were created by the same deity, why not allow us all to live forever in Paradise? Besides, would an avid birdwatcher consider it Paradise if there were no birds? Would someone who spent their life rescuing cats, dogs, and other animals see it as Heaven if there were no animals to thank them and share love eternally? To further understand the concept of *animal souls*, let's look at it scientifically.

The Science Behind the Soul

For a long time it was said that it is impossible to prove the existence of souls in people, let alone animals. That is until recently. Doctors at the NYU Grossman School of Medicine are researching a phenomenon that cannot be scientifically explained—a continued consciousness while being resuscitated. Although claims of consciousness after passing away were earlier dismissed and explained as being hallucinations, or the brain going haywire as life leaves the body, further studies are now proving the contrary.

A Study on Consciousness

Doctor Sam Parnia explains that when a person dies the first thing that happens is the heart stops beating. When the heart has stopped, breathing also stops which means there is no oxygen being carried to the rest of the body, including the brain. According to Doctor Parnia, this is enough cause to declare that a person has passed away. Still, a person who has passed away *can* be brought back to life in minutes or longer, through the process of resuscitation. This means that the person's spirit or life force can return to the body.

What this implies is that a person does not simply cease to exist when they have passed away. There must be something that continues to exist that can be brought back to the body, and bring that person back to life. Of course, not all attempts at resuscitation are successful,

86

therefore the study was done on cases where a person had clinically died and was revived.

During the last decades, millions of people have come forward to report what happened to them when they passed away, before they were brought back to life. Some people reported continued awareness of their surroundings, even though their brain activity completely stopped, while others report near-death experiences. People who claimed to have been aware between the period of passing and reviving stated that they knew what everyone was doing and what was happening, as they could see and hear everything. Doctor Parnia adds that this is not possible from the scientific point of view. Consciousness, according to science, is situated in the brain, therefore, if the brain does not function, there should be no consciousness.

Thankfully the doctors at NYU Grossman School of Medicine found this so interesting that they could not let it go. They had to know more and want to understand this phenomenon. By 2017, no less than 15 medical centers have decided to take part in this study. Once a study was completed on 2,000 people, they found that 40% of these people who had passed and were revived reported that they were consciously aware of what was going on around them. This included what people, such as medical staff and doctors, said and what happened during the time the subjects should not have had awareness at all. Many of these people could describe in incredible detail what was going on while they had passed away.

Doctors find this intriguing, as this is proof of consciousness after passing, something which is scientifically impossible. The only solution is that our consciousness does not rely merely on the functioning of our brain and does not cease to exist once a person has passed away. This is tangible proof that every person has a soul, which is our conscious part that will never cease to exist.

Doctor Parnia stated that they now have evidence that consciousness, awareness, or the psyche does not cease to exist after passing away. He also said that people have been revived after having passed for hours. People who had near-death experiences are often impacted profoundly, with this experience changing their lives. These people describe seeing a bright light, feeling loved, warm, and secure, and often seeing relatives who had passed away. Some tell of a *life review*, where they saw their life and all the choices they made, gaining insight and a new perspective.

These people return, not fearing death anymore, being more helpful and kind, and finding true purpose in living. A near-death experience changes a person completely. I believe this is why some people are allowed this experience. This cannot be ascribed to hallucinations, as a functioning brain is required to hallucinate. At the point where people experience awareness or near-death experiences, their brain was not functioning at all. This means that our consciousness can and will operate without our bodies. The question now is, why do only 10% of people have near-death experiences? Doctor Parnia explained that he believes everyone experiences the same thing. However, after a person is revived, they are given medication to minimize possible harm to the brain. This neurological medication causes memory loss, which means many people who do see the light and relatives who have passed away forgot about their experience, because of the medication (Parnia et al., 2014).

How Can We Prove that Animals Have Souls?

Any pet-parent will say with assurance that their pets do have souls. But those who don't love animals as much as we do may argue that there is no proof. Can we prove that animals do have souls? Yes, we can. How do we know that humans have souls? Is it because of something we learned while growing up, or is it because of personal or spiritual experience? The human soul is linked to consciousness—the fact that humans have a will, levels of intellect, and emotions. To imply that animals have none of these is problematic.

Anyone who does not believe that animals have souls must begin taking dogs for a walk. Every so often you'll find a dog that plops to the ground, refusing to move. You can try begging, threats, or offering them bribes, but if a dog decided they don't want to walk, they likely won't. Is this not proof that the dog has a will of their own? Even cats or any other animal cannot be forced to play or do anything they don't *want* to do. Why would there be a saying such as *Being as stubborn as a mule*? This indicates free will, one of the attributes of a soul.

Let's consider levels of intellect in the animal kingdom. People speak of their pets, especially dogs, who would *know* when it is time for their owners to come home. They would go to the gate or door and wait for their owners to arrive. Or pets that know when it's time to eat will act accordingly, coming to the place where they get their food or making noise at their bowls. But let's get more daring and talk about insects. Bees do a waggle dance to communicate the locations of flowers to other bees. Wow, that's smart! What makes it even more impressive, is that if another bee had difficulty in the area of these flowers, such as encountering spiders, they will interrupt the bee performing the dance, as if to say, *Whoa, dude, we can't go there! There are spiders!* There are wasps who recognize other wasps by their face. This means that facial recognition is not limited to beings of higher intellect, but proof of intellect even in the kingdom of insects. It is clear then that animals have their own will and show levels of intellect. But what about the third attribute, which is emotions?

Think about a dog again, waiting for their owner to come home. How do they react when they see their pet-parent? Do they stare emotionlessly and walk on like an emotionless robot? No, the dog is excited and clearly happy. Their tail is wagging, their breathing increases, and some dogs will make sounds accompanying their excitement. What else is this than emotion? Being affectionate is also not limited to human experience. Pets can be highly affectionate. Cats and dogs often look for attention and will do anything to draw your attention to them. Just as they thrive on being loved, they return gestures of love to their pet-parents. Cats will lay on your lap and purr or wrap their tail around your leg, dogs will lick your hand, and birds will put their heads snug against your face, which all are proof of emotion.

Besides, animals get angry, sad, and scared too. When humans have these experiences, we call them emotions. Why call it anything else simply because it is experienced by animals? Therefore, we have proven that animals have free will, show levels of intellect, and live for displays of emotion. In turn, this proves that animals do have souls. I believe that many people are not willing to acknowledge that animals have souls, so they won't feel guilty about what is being done to nature and all her animals.

Wild Souls

It may be easy to argue that *pets act like their owners*, a case of monkey see, monkey do. But what about animals in the wild? Do they have souls? Or are only animals loved by pet-parents destined to have souls? Let's take a look at what is happening in the wild, and if it is possible for wild animals to have consciousness.

You don't need to be a wildlife expert to know that animals in the wild share many traits with us—they nurture their young, can be playful, understand when to run and when to fight, and seek companionship. Status is important to animals too. Animals will often fight for the status of leader. How does one animal become the leader? The others yield to their leadership. Does this not suggest a high level of consciousness? This means that animals can see and calculate for themselves who is fit enough to be their leader.

Similar to the way animals can identify their leaders, they also know who their enemies and friends are, understand the importance of sheltering themselves, know that they need food, especially their young, and understand what to do to survive. Animals are not very different from us, are they? Consciousness implies having a mental experience. For example, if you go to a vending machine and deposit a coin to buy a soft drink, the machine reacts to the coin you have deposited and the button you pushed by *giving* you a soft drink. Does this mean the vending machine knows what it is doing? Of course not. It is not learning anything. Imagine going to a vending machine and the next thing you know it is stretching out a hand to take your money.

Those who say that animals do not have souls or consciousness think of animals as *vending machines*. Animated flesh and bone machines without thought, will, or emotions. We simply can't agree to this. The widespread assumption that animals do not have souls stem from science, as they could not confirm consciousness in animals. Since they could not confirm it, they simply stated that animals could not have consciousness. But this is a wild assumption that has taken root and grown over the years. Had the consciousness of animals been accepted earlier on, there might have been less animal testing, poaching, or abuse.

Wildlife researchers and rangers often have names for animals in the wild. They can distinguish between different elephants, lions, or other animals by their appearance, but you will often hear them say, *This lion is very playful, but his brother is lazy,* or *This elephant is a strict mother, but her sister is kinder to the calves.* This means that these researchers and rangers associate each animal with their own unique personality. If these animals in the wild have personalities where there is little human interaction, how can anyone think a *pet* can't have a personality? I'm sure you have had pets with numerous personalities! All that is left is to agree that a personality and soul go hand-in-hand.

It's Only Human to Have Empathy, Right?

Carl Safina (2015) says that animals do express empathy toward one another. He tells of an old woman who got lost in the wild. She couldn't see well, so her family was terribly worried. They found her the next day within a sort of cage built with branches. There were also elephants close by, seemingly protecting her. She told them that there were hyenas that wanted her, but the elephants protected her and built the cage around her using branches. Amazing, isn't it? But please, don't go try and pat the nearest elephant on the head. They choose who they trust, which happens rarely.

People have seen humpback whales protect seals from becoming an oceanic predator's lunch. In one such documented case, a humpback whale spotted a seal that was being chased by two killer whales. The humpback whale swept the seal on their back out of the water, safe from the killer whales. Similarly, there are accounts of dolphins saving people from sharks. This means that these animals are able to commit acts that will be of no benefit to themselves. That's empathy, something one can only possess if they have a soul.

Strangely Familiar

When you have a pet you spend a lot of time with, you get to know their quirks, likes, and dislikes. Pets have different things they do, for example, a dog may like to carry around the television set's remote control, fetch the newspaper in the mornings, or go crazy whenever you touch the leash before you take them for a walk. Cats may like to push things off shelves, use the same window to exit and enter the house, or have a favorite sleeping spot. In the same way, any pet has things they do - habits unique to the pet.

When your pet passes away, you keep on thinking about these quirks and habits. Why? Because these were the things that made them special and unique. Also, because these are the things you are going to miss the most. It is then that the grieving starts, which is a very hard time to deal with. Some people decide to never get a pet again, while others can't wait to find a new pet-child on whom they can pour all of their love. Some people claim that after adopting a new pet, they often recognize things that are strangely familiar. There may be things about the new pet that reminds them of their pet that has passed away. I'm not talking about a dog wagging their tail, all of them do this, but the unique traits of the animal that has transitioned that are shared with the new pet.

How is this possible? There is only one answer—your beloved pet has reincarnated because they want to be with you. I believe that similarly to people, most pets may not be aware that they are reincarnated. I think that this awareness only takes place in the realm of the spirit. Therefore, it is possible that some of your pets are reincarnations of your pets that have transitioned.

Thankfully there are ways to tell if your pet was reincarnated. People believe that pets choose when and how to be reincarnated. This idea comes from the claims of people who say that they have been reincarnated, and chose to come back. I once read about a young boy who told his mother that he *chose* her to be his mother. He said that he was watching her from Heaven, and decided that he wanted no one else but her to be his mother. He then told in amazing detail about his previous life. The child was around four years old. When they looked into his story, they found a person matching the description he gave to the finest detail. However, this person passed away more than a century before the boy was born.

It does the grieving heart good to know that your pets may come back to you, either in spirit or often being reincarnated. Be aware, however, that reincarnation does not mean your pet will be a clone of the pet that has passed. Your new pet will have their own personality, but you will be aware of similarities shared with your passed pet. Just like some people may remember parts of their past lives, pets may too. Since your new pet will have a different personality, your relationship with them won't be the same as with your pet that has crossed over. But this isn't a bad thing. Every relationship you have with a pet can be beautiful and memorable.

Some people believe that pets may reincarnate as the same species while others will come back as a different species and that they may choose to change their gender when reincarnated. You may have communicated with your pet, or made use of a pet communicator where your pet told you themselves that they want to join you in the physical world again. This is wonderful because then you know for sure your pet will be reincarnated, waiting for you to find them. You can then decide if you want them to come back as the same species, breed, or sex, and when you want them to reincarnate. It may sound like you would be demanding, but remember that your pet wants to see you happy and pleased, and will therefore easily agree to the things you desire.

Let's say, for example, you had a German shepherd as you had children in the house. You knew that a German shepherd is the best dog to have when you have children. Years have come and gone, and your German shepherd has passed away, but your children are both grown and out of the house. Would you need a German shepherd again? Maybe you would prefer a rottweiler, as you are more in need of a guard dog. You can ask your pet to reincarnate as a rottweiler. Don't worry, they won't be offended. If you know a specific breeder you like and know that they are terrific with animals, you can ask your pet to be reincarnated into this breeder's care. Your pet will be too happy and eager to fulfill your needs. It is not a question of them coming back as *perfect* for them to be happy, as long as they come back, their happiness will be fulfilled.

If you want your pet to reincarnate but you are unable to communicate with them, you can visualize all your needs, imagine creating an energy orb placing all your needs in there, and then release it to the universe. Your pet will receive it, as long as your intention is strong and pure. Once you've done this, don't sit back and wait for your pet to come back to you on their own. Go out and look for them. You will receive signs to know where you should go and what you should do. A certain pet store may draw your attention, or you may feel strongly toward a certain breeder.

Perhaps while you are going through a newspaper, words may seem to be highlighted, demanding your focus. Pay attention, this part in the newspaper may be telling you where to look for your reincarnated pet. If you feel strongly that you should travel and you decide to do so, look around at the place you have traveled to. It may be that your pet has reincarnated to this location and is trying to make you aware that they were born in that specific location.

It may be hard to comprehend as the spiritual realm is vast and complex, but when your pet is reincarnated it is their soul that is reborn. Their spirit is still in the afterlife, which means that should you pass away before your reincarnated pet does, their spirit will still be waiting for you at the Rainbow Bridge.

Real Accounts of Reincarnation

In January of 2017, Tatiana Vaske's beloved dog Baloo passed away. He was only 11 months old. His passing was sudden and for Tatiana, it felt like this was the hardest thing she ever had to deal with. She kept telling everyone that Baloo will come back to her and she believes that he did. Tatiana is certain that her new dog is her transitioned Baloo's reincarnated soul. She felt that Baloo, who had passed, was her soul mate. The month before she adopted her new dog she had dreams about Baloo. These dreams were recurring, and Tatiana felt like Baloo was trying to communicate something. The strange thing is that she dreamt Baloo came back as a girl. She thought this was not possible, as Baloo was a boy.

After the dreams, she found a young lady who was selling Saint Bernard puppies on Twitter. When she viewed the photos of the puppies, she noticed that one puppy had a black spot on top of their head, identical to what Baloo looked like. When she communicated with Baloo before, she told him that when he is reincarnated, she will recognize him from a black spot on his head. Tatiana asked the young lady if she had any male puppies to which the young lady replied that they were all girls.

She was hesitant at first, but a friend advised her to go and see the puppies. Tatiana went to see the puppies. While all of the puppies were acting normal, one puppy came right up to her to sleep on her lap. Can you guess which puppy it was? Of course, the one with the black spot on her head! Tatiana also realized that the day she went to see the puppies was the same day of the month Baloo had passed away. Also, she saw the puppies 11 months after Baloo's passing, which is the age Baloo was when he passed.

The first day Tatiana brought the puppy to her home, she immediately ran to the bathroom. It was like the puppy knew the layout of the house, without ever seeing or having to learn it. One night the puppy kept barking at a laundry basket that was filled with clothes. Tatiana wanted to see what the puppy was barking at, so she picked up the clothes, only to find a toy bone Baloo loved to play with. When the puppy saw the toy bone, she stopped fussing and was all too happy to have the bone. Tatiana said that the toy bone was hidden and there was no way for the puppy to have seen it. According to Tatiana, the puppy has many characteristics Baloo had and very similar quirks. She decided to name the new puppy Baloo (Vaske, 2017).

Pet psychic Teresa Wagner tells of a lady who had lost her dog tragically and then came to Teresa for help. They communicated with her beloved dog who then told them that he would be reincarnated. He told them the date and location the lady would find him. She went to the shelter she was told to go to, where she was drawn to a large white dog. The moment she looked into the dog's eyes, there was an instant loving connection. She knew that this must be the reincarnation of her beloved dog. On their way home, she started crying, as she suddenly had doubts. What if this was not her transitioned dog's reincarnation? What if she made a mistake?

She pulled off the road and turned to the dog who was sitting next to her. She told the dog that she loved him and would take care of him forever, but she just wanted a sign that he was her beloved old dog. The dog then got up on his hind legs and wrapped his front legs around her neck. This was astounding, as this was something her transitioned dog would often do. She then knew without a shadow of a doubt that this was the reincarnation of her old dog (Wagner, 2006).

Andreana Dorrs, who is an animal communicator, has a very compelling story to tell. She loves horses, and from the moment she first saw Ebony knew that they were meant to be together. Andreana says that Ebony is a gentle, true, and honest horse. Ebony was a bit unbalanced and got extremely nervous whenever someone tried to ride her. Although Andreana knew that there was more to this, it did not bother her. As long as they could be together, she was content.

Andreana met a psychic lady who offered to do a past life regression with Andreana, to which she agreed. During the session, Andreana had memories of a past life. Andreana remembered that she and Ebony had spent a lifetime together in Germany many years ago. Ebony was a prize mare and loved to be ridden. Ebony and Andreana loved each other as much as they love each other today. But one day there was an accident—as they were riding, they slipped down a ravine. Ebony fell on her back on top of Andreana. The impact broke Ebony's back and she passed away instantly. Andreana was trapped under her with a broken pelvis and passed two days later.

Although the story may seem tragic, Andreana felt grateful, as she now understood why she had such a deep connection with Ebony. Still, Andreana felt guilty for her past self riding Ebony that close to the ridge. She didn't tell anyone about the past life regression. But then a friend of hers, who is also an animal communicator, had to see Andreana as she was certain Ebony was trying to communicate with her. She told Andreana that she had to pull over, as she kept seeing images that Ebony was projecting to her mind.

This lady went on to tell Andreana that her horse felt sorry for falling on her which ultimately caused them both to pass away. Ebony was hoping that Andreana did not blame her for their passing, as it was an accident. Andreana said that after that, and with the help of the animal communicator, they could figure things out and deal with trauma together. Since then, Ebony loves to be ridden and is becoming more confident every day (Dorrs, 2013).

Chapter 6

True Testimonies of Love and Healing

Our souls speak a language that is beyond human understanding.
A connection so rare the universe won't let us part
—Nikki Rowe (Goodreads, n.d.).

Will I Ever Heal From This?

The loss of one of your pet-children is traumatic and devastating. There are several stages of grief, but we won't be getting into any of that. Let's face it—this grief can make you feel helpless, emotionally paralyzed, angry, and depressed. If guilt is paired with these emotions, it makes dealing with it agonizing. Still, we have learned that the spirit world is very real. In fact, many people who had the opportunity to see this world described it as being even more real than the physical world. The most comforting thing about all this is knowing that our beloved pets that have transitioned come to visit us, leave us messages to help us heal, and will often choose to be

101

reincarnated. Why? Because they love us. This love is eternal, unbreakable, and healing in itself.

From the Hearts of Pet-Parents

In this section, we'll be talking about true accounts of people being visited by their pets from the afterlife. These visitations and messages brought them hope, healing, and comfort.

Before we get to other people's stories, I'd like to tell you about things I personally experienced. Remember Larry? This story involves him. I invited Larry to accompany me to visit some friends of mine, Tina and Martin, who were people he had never met. I didn't tell him anything about them. My intention was a casual visit, but the universe had different plans. When we arrived, I noticed that Larry kept looking at the ground, as if he was following something. However, my friends' cat and dog were not close to where he was looking.

Because I've known Larry since we were children, I could read the look on his face. I knew that he was seeing *something*. We took our seats in the living room and talked, but Larry was quiet. This happens when a spirit is trying to get his attention. Out of the blue Larry asked Tina if she had a black and white tomcat. It looked like he took the wind right out of her sails. She answered that she did. He then told her that he only passed away two weeks ago, which she confirmed. He then said, *He likes climbing on the back of your chair, lying down behind your head, and sleeping with his head on your shoulder.* She began to cry. This was her cat's favorite place to sleep.

Although I shouldn't be surprised at Larry's gift anymore, I was baffled. He had no way of knowing. But it didn't end here. He then continued to say, *He doesn't blame you. He asked to go out, and you let him. He had to go out. He knew it was his time.* Tina cried even harder. She had let her cat, Tom, out of the house, because he asked her to go out. He wandered too close to the street when a driver went off the road and onto the curb, only for the purpose of ending Tom's life. Larry continued, *Tom knew that he was ill and that he was going to suffer. This was the only way he could be free from pain and suffering. Don't blame yourself or hate the driver. Tom is with you, and will always be.*

Martin and I joined in the tear fest. Larry then said, *Don't neglect your other pets, thinking that it is unfair that Tom is missing out on love and attention. He is filled with love, and your parents are giving him attention every moment.* Tina laughed. Just like her, her parents used to love rescuing animals. She knew that they would take good care of Tom. She was relieved. By the end of the evening, we were all laughing again. Tina thanked me for bringing Larry along. I apologized for all the tears, to which Tina replied that the tears were necessary. *How else would I heal?* she asked. She understood that Tom's passing was not an accident—it was providence.

The Grieving Pet-Dad

After Carlos Sluzki's cat passed away, he kept seeing his cat, but only from the corner of his eye. He would see his cat at any time during the day, regardless of how hectic the day was. Carlos began to realize that his cat was fading as days went by as he was succeeding in dealing with his grief. Once he had dealt with his grief to the extent that he could continue his life normally, he did not see his cat again (Bell, 2008). His cat was looking after him, checking in to see if their pet-parent was okay. What love they had shared!

Wiggie's Warning

Debra Tadman, who is a nursery school teacher, had a cat named Wiggie. Wiggie was with his pet-parent through many difficult times. When he passed away, Debra was devastated. She felt like she lost a child. Wanting to find solace, she contacted an animal communicator, Sharon Callaghan, to talk to her beloved pet. To Debra's great relief, Sharon was able to make contact with Wiggie. The cat gave Debra a stern warning—he was worried about her apartment being a *toxic place*. At first, neither Sharon nor Debra knew what the cat meant.

A year after their meeting, Debra decided to paint her apartment. To her surprise, she found asbestos and toxic mold. She immediately understood that this was what Wiggie warned her about. Sharon had no way of knowing since the mold and asbestos were hidden inside the walls of Debra's apartment. This brought Debra comfort and a feeling of gratefulness toward Wiggie. He was still looking out for Debra, even from the afterlife.

Let's Play Ball

Yabba was Maureen's beloved dog but sadly passed away 11 days before her birthday. Maureen woke up suddenly and realized that Yabba had passed away during the night. Maureen was in deep sorrow and described Yabba as being her rock. The moment she saw that her dog had passed away, Maureen grabbed her camera in the hopes of getting a photograph of Yabba's spirit. In one of the photos, Maureen was certain she saw the shape of her beloved Yabba.

After this, Maureen made a memorial using a rosary, candle, and some of Yabba's favorite toys. Some time after this she took out a ball and placed it on the ground. She then told Yabba that she wanted to play with her. Suddenly the ball rolled *all on its own*. Maureen knew that Yabba was with her. Then the ball moved again. At that moment Maureen felt Yabba brushing against her. She knew that her dog was with her, telling her that she was well and that she will always be with Maureen (Marcano, 2021).

A Dream of Fields

Barbara Mercy had a beautiful border collie named Glen. From the moment they adopted Glen, he preferred not to sleep on his doggy bed, but rather on a blanket in the stairwell. They would hear their door open every morning as Glen pushed it open. He would then go to Barbara's side of the bed to greet her. She would then give him a loving pat on his head. After this, Glen would go to Barbara's husband's side to say *good morning*. Glen passed away when he was 15 years old. Barbara says that she and her husband were distraught after Glen's passing.

The morning after his passing, Barbara heard the bedroom door opening. She said to her husband, momentarily forgetting that Glen had passed away, *Glen's here*. Barbara let her hand off the bed and patted Glen on his head. She could feel her dog's fur, and then it faded while she was touching him. It was a reminder that their dog had passed, but still, also a reminder that he was still with them. That night Barbara had a dream about Glen. She saw him running over green fields with other dogs. This gave her comfort. She knew that Glen was free, at peace, but most importantly, he was happy.

No amount of words can take away the pain that comes with the loss of a pet. All I can say is that we never truly get over the loss, we learn to live with it and embrace the moments we had with our pets. With this, we have the comfort of knowing we will be reunited with them someday, meeting them at the Rainbow Bridge. After that comes an eternity of playing, laughing, and embracing. We may experience sadness now, but the joy that will fill us on the day we transition will wipe away every last tear, and we will be given a never-ending supply of comforting light, peace, love, and the joy of being with our beloved pet-children.

Conclusion

What we have enjoyed, we can never lose.
All that we love deeply becomes a part of us
— Helen Keller (Butler 2022).

The loss of a pet causes devastating grief, feelings of helplessness, and often depression. This book, *Yes, Pets do Go to Heaven* answers questions such as:

⊙ Does my pet have a soul?

⊙ Is my pet in Heaven?

⊙ Can I still talk to my pet?

⊙ Will my pet come back to me in physical form?

The answer to all these questions, as was discussed in this book, is yes! There is comfort in knowing that our beloved pets will always be with us, in this life and the world behind the veil, and that they will communicate with us. We all know that the Catholic Church honors several patron saints. One of these saints is St. Francis. Who is he? He is the patron saint of animals. If animals did not have a spirit or soul, why would St. Francis be their patron saint? This can only mean that animals are precious and have a place on earth and in Heaven.

In Chapter 1, we examined the souls of animals. We saw that people had pets as far as 32,000 years ago. Animals were greatly revered by ancient cultures. Most of these cultures believed that animals had souls and would exist in the afterlife. The ancients cared deeply for their pets and treated them exceptionally well. The Greeks viewed the harming of an animal as equal to harming a member of your own family. Many Egyptians had their pets mummified to prepare them for the afterlife.

In 2020, Pope Francis declared that people must respect nature, as we will one day share Paradise with nature and all her creatures. We also discussed what Heaven is like for our transitioned pets. We have found that Heaven is different for each pet. It is the same place, but caters to every pet's likes and loves. We then saw fascinating stories about people who had near-death experiences, people who testified that they saw pets in the afterlife.

In Chapter 2, we talked about what happens to our pets when they pass away. We also talked about grief and how it may affect us. We then considered the possibility that our pets are still aware of us once they have transitioned. We came to the conclusion that they do, and want us to know that they still think about us, love us, and want to protect us. The connection between a pet and their owner is powerful. They are bound by love, which is a bond that will never break. When a pet transitions, their experience is very similar to ours. They feel free, loved, and warmth.

We then asked the question: if our pets are happy in Paradise, why would they *want* to come and visit us? They come to us to communicate because they love us. The love between a pet-parent and their pet-children will never end. Our pets know when we are sad. They want us to be happy. This is why they give us signs and messages. They want us to heal and be full of joy again. We also saw that pets are indeed psychic. They have intuitive knowledge about things such as thunderstorms, natural disasters, and strangers coming to our homes. Therefore, they don't find it hard to communicate with us.

In Chapter 3, we saw that we need to be sensitive to signs and messages from our pets. The messages may sometimes be subtle, so we need to pay close attention to our surroundings. Before communicating with a transitioned pet, try communicating with a pet in the physical world first. You first need to visualize the message. Know exactly what you want to say. Practice by saying this out loud. Get your emotions and mind in sync. The energy of your message must be balanced and strong. When you are ready, talk to your pet and give them your message, and then watch if their behavior changes.

When you are ready to communicate with your transitioned pet, you need to calm your mind first. Then you can follow the steps suggested in Chapter 3 to protect yourself. Remember to develop your clairvoyance, clairaudience, clairsentience, and claircognizance. Clairvoyance is your ability to see the spiritual realm, clairaudience is when you can hear messages or sounds from spirits, clairsentience is feeling things from beyond the veil, while claircognizance is knowing things in a supernatural way.

In Chapter 4, we examined signs, symbols, and messages from the spiritual plane. We first looked at how these signs were interpreted in history. We then discussed how you can find signs by looking for them, such as seeing the spirit of your beloved pet, interpreting dreams about your transitioned pet, acknowledging sudden memories of your time with your pet, hearing sounds that may be your pet trying to communicate, feeling your pet's presence physically, or smelling something that can't be explained but reminds you of your pet.

We then talked about how you can deal with grief after losing a pet. Write down all the emotions you are experiencing. Look at these emotions. Feeling sad, lonely, or devastated is normal. We all go through these emotions. But if there are feelings such as resentment or guilt, you must deal with them quickly. Resentment and guilt will not help your healing process, but may only make the pain worse. Your pet doesn't want you to feel guilt or resentment. They want you to keep on loving and remembering them without feeling the need to punish yourself. They just want you to heal and be happy. Paying attention to messages from your pet will fill you with hope, making the bond between you and your pet stronger.

In Chapter 5, we discussed reincarnation. We answered the question of whether your pet will return to the physical world. Ultimately, it is your pet's choice. But more often than not pets choose to reincarnate. We looked at the beliefs of different cultures and religions, where we found that many religions do believe in reincarnation. We then examined the concept of the soul in humans and animals. We saw that even wild animals share many of our characteristics—they love, fear, know when to fight, when to run away, seek shelter, and find food. They understand caring for their young, and show affection. They have their own will, high levels of intellect, and are capable of showing emotion, which are all traits of having a soul.

We then learned how to look for signs that your pet was reincarnated. You may feel drawn to a pet store, have strong feelings about a certain breeder, have your attention drawn to something in a newspaper, or feel the need to travel to a certain location. Whichever way, these may be messages from your pet to come and find them. Next, we read true stories about reincarnation and how it changed people's lives.

In Chapter 6, we talked about true accounts of people being visited by their beloved pets after they have transitioned. These visitations brought their pet-parents comfort, hope, and peace. Many people came to the understanding that their pets are happy and loved in the afterlife. We also learned that our pets never leave our side. They are close to us in spirit or embraced by us as reincarnated souls. Whichever way, our pets are watching over us while we are still in the physical world.

Don't be afraid to communicate with your pet. They want you to hear from them, and in the same way, want to hear from you. Receiving messages from your pets is comforting, and will allow the healing process to start. Consider those who never had pets. I know several people who have never had pets, and I am sure you do also. Even though I have lost pets I am grateful—I had the chance to love deeply and unconditionally. Do you feel the same gratitude? I hope that you do. The point is, that deep and unconditional love will never fade. *Never.* In the end, when we close our eyes for the last time, we will walk into the comforting light, right up to the Rainbow Bridge. There we will meet our beloved pets to share love, laughter, and a world where nothing can separate us for eternity, in a new Paradise existing specially for us.

If you have found this book to be interesting, insightful, helpful, or comforting, kindly leave a fitting review.

May you be blessed!

References

ABC Science. (2020, November 10). *Guided Meditation For Calming The Mind (5 Minutes) | Natural Mindful.* YouTube. https://www.youtube.com/watch?v=zUOGeHJjkU8

Abercrombie, S. (2014, December 16). *A light in the darkness of the botched pope-animal story.* National Catholic Reporter; EarthBeat. https://www.ncronline.org/blogs/earthbeat/eco-catholic/light-darkness-botched-pope-animal-story

Alexander, E. (2012). *Proof of Heaven: A Neurosurgeon's Journey into the Afterlife.* Simon & Schuster.

American Institute of Physics. (2018, May 21). *A better way to control crystal vibrations: By introducing impurities to a material, researchers can control the speed and frequency of phonons, potentially leading to more energy-efficient devices.* ScienceDaily. https://www.sciencedaily.com/releases/2018/05/180521154243.htm#:~:text=The%20vibrational%20motion%20of%20an

Annus, A., Rochberg, F., & Allen, J. (2010). *Divination and Interpretation of Signs in the Ancient World* (U. S. Koch, Ed.). The University of Chicago.

Baron-Reid, C. (2008). *Messages from Spirit: The Extraordinary Power of Oracles, Omens, and Signs.* Hay House.

Beauregard, M., & O'Leary, D. (2007). *The Spiritual Brain: A Neuroscientist's Case for the Existence of the Soul.* HarperCollins.

Bell, V. (2008, December 2). *Ghost Stories: Visits from the Deceased.* Scientific American. https://www.scientificamerican.com/article/ghost-stories-visits-from-the-deceased/

Bulğen, M. (2018). *Reincarnation (Tanāsukh) According to Islam: Comparative, Historical and Contemporary Analyses.* Reincarnation, *1*(1). https://doi.org/10.5281/zenodo.1488657

Butler, T. (2022, February 2). *60 Sympathetic Pet Loss Quotes.* LoveToKnow. https://dying.lovetoknow.com/Loss_of_a_Pet_Quotes

Carter, C. (2010). *Science and the Near-Death Experience: How Consciousness Survives Death.* Inner Traditions.

Charbonier, J. J. (2015). *7 Reasons to Believe in the Afterlife: A Doctor Reviews the Case for Consciousness after Death.* Inner Traditions.

Cherokee Billie Spiritual Advisor. (2019). *What Your Deceased Pet Wants You To Know After Life! By Cherokee Billie.* YouTube. https://www.youtube.com/watch?v=Pofe4riUUco&list=PLc wdG7zJ3TB1WStPayAwv9Uf9ZRNGU2GG

Chestney, K. (2017, June 13). *Beyond Saints & Psychics: Why Enlightenment is for Everyone.* Intuit or Die. https://medium.com/intuit-or-die/beyond-saints-psychics-why-enlightenment-is-for-everyone-55249a46d49c

Communicate with Angels. (2020, December 23). *Develop your Gift of Clairaudience.* YouTube. https://www.youtube.com/watch?v=wOMWcYl220E

Danchevskaya, O. Y. (n.d.). *Concept of Soul among North American Indians* (pp. 89–96). Retrieved March 22, 2022, from https://www.se.edu/international-student/wp-content/uploads/sites/85/2019/09/NAS-2011-Proceedings-Danchevskaya.pdf

Das, S. (2019, February 20). *Quotes About Reincarnation.* Learn Religions. https://www.learnreligions.com/quotes-on-reincarnation-1770558

Dicastero per la Comunicazione. (2020, September 1). *Message of the Holy Father for the World Day of Prayer for the Care of Creation | Francis.* Www.vatican.va; Libreria Editrice Vaticana. https://www.vatican.va/content/francesco/en/messages/pont-messages/2020/documents/papa-francesco_20200901_messaggio-giornata-cura-creato.html

Donna. (2022). *Do dogs have souls? And will my dog go to heaven?* (J. Mitchell, Ed.). Boston Terrier Network. https://bostonterriernetwork.com/index.php/category-blog/617-do-dogs-have-souls-and-will-my-dog-do-to-heaven.html

Dorrs, A. (2013, February 16). *Remember Me - Past Life with my horse.* Of Horse! https://www.ofhorse.com/view-post/Remember-Me-Past-Life-with-my-horse

Duke, B. (2015, January 5). *10 Biblical Truths About Animals.* The Ethics and Religious Liberty Commission. https://erlc.com/resource-library/articles/10-biblical-truths-about-animals/

Eaton, B. (2013). *Afterlife: Uncovering the Secrets of Life After Death.* Jeremy P. Tarcher/Penguin.

Fitzpatrick, S. (2020, September 24). *Saying Goodbye To Your Pet A Guide To Help You Through Bereavement by Sonya Fitzpatrick.* YouTube. https://www.youtube.com/watch?v=LepaLChPfp4

Forever in My Heart. (2016, August 24). *Ancient Civilizations and Pets.* Forever in My Heart Jewelry. https://foreverinmyheartjewelry.com/blogs/news/ancient-civilizations-and-pets

Fraser, M. (2022, February 9). *Pet Heaven & The Afterlife.* YouTube. https://www.youtube.com/watch?v=3wL6TV8JkOE&t=52s

Fridono, J. (n.d.). *Reincarnation in dogs.* Surf Dog Ricochet. Retrieved March 22, 2022, from https://www.surfdogricochet.com/reincarnation-in-pets.html

Heart, V. (2017). *Revealed! Hidden Secrets To Communicating With Pets: Learn How to Connect and Send Messages to Animals.* Heart Communication Enterprises Inc. https://learnhowtotalktoanimals.com/wp-content/uploads/2015/11/Hidden-Secrets-to-Communicating-with-Pets-v2.pdf

Heaven is For Real Ministries. (2018). *Frequently Asked Questions.* Heaven Is for Real Ministries. https://www.heavenlive.org/faq

Hollister, K. (2018, July 7). *Grief is Like The Ocean.* Elevate Counseling Services. https://www.elevate-counseling.com/grief-is-like-the-ocean/#:~:text=%E2%80%9CGrief%20is%20like%20the%20ocean

Hopler, W. (2018, May 3). *Signs and Messages From Animals in the Afterlife*. Learn Religions. https://www.learnreligions.com/afterlife-signs-and-messages-from-animals-124096

Hopler, W. (2019, June 25). *Do Animals Go to Heaven? Afterlife Animal Miracles*. Learn Religions. https://www.learnreligions.com/afterlife-animal-miracles-and-heaven-124097

Ingram, L. (2020, August 17). *312 Heartwarming Quotes About Fur-ever Love That Will Make You Want to Hug Your Pet*. Parade. https://parade.com/867535/leahingram/51-awesome-adorable-and-inspirational-quotes-about-pets-for-national-pet-day-2019/

James Van Praagh. (2017). *Wisdom from Your Spirit Guides: A Handbook to Contact Your Soul's Greatest Teachers*. Hay House.

Jayaram, V. (2019). *The Significance of Animals in Hinduism*. Hinduwebsite.com. https://www.hinduwebsite.com/hinduism/h_animals.asp

Joe, J. (2022, January 11). *Ancient Egypt's Animals: How the Egyptians Tamed the Wilderness*. Timeless Myth; Elite CafeMedia. https://www.timelessmyths.com/history/ancient-egypts-animals/

Johnson, S. (2021, June 30). *These 5 Religions Believe in Animal or Pet Reincarnation | Cake Blog*. Cake. https://www.joincake.com/blog/animal-reincarnation/

Katz, D. L. (2008). *Extraordinary Psychic: Proven Techniques to Master Your Natural Psychic Abilities*. Llewellyn Publications.

Kessler, S. (2021, April 6). *20 Common Claims of Signs From Deceased Pets | Cake Blog. Cake.*
https://www.joincake.com/blog/signs-from-deceased-pets/

Lerma, J. (2007). *Into the Light: Real Life Stories about Angelic Visits, Visions of the Afterlife, and Other Pre-death Experiences*. New Page Books.

Long, J., & Perry, P. (2010). *Evidence of the Afterlife: The Science of Near-Death Experiences*. HarperCollins.

Lynn McKenzie Animal Communicator, Healer & Psychic. (2018, June 1). *Animal Reincarnation and How to Find Them Once They've Returned*. YouTube.
https://www.youtube.com/watch?v=lYyeWC59iuY

MacKinnon, D. (2019, April 3). *What does my pet do in Heaven? What Happens When Animals Go to the Other Side?* YouTube.
https://www.youtube.com/watch?v=lJFiJCtBWeM

MacKinnon, D. (2020, May 24). *3 Things to do for pet loss and pet grief | Animal Afterlife & Rainbow Bridge*. YouTube.
https://www.youtube.com/watch?v=KsPldyw1ybI

Mannes, E. (2018). *Soul Dog: A Journey Into the Spiritual Life of Animals*. Bear & Company.

Marcano, S. (2021, September 23). *11 Pets Who Returned As Ghosts To Help Or Haunt Their Owners*. Ranker.
https://www.ranker.com/list/pets-who-returned-as-ghosts/scottmarcano

Marisa Grieco - Your Mystical Guide. (2018, March 14). *4 Tips to Develop Your Clairvoyant Superpower.* YouTube. https://www.youtube.com/watch?v=dWFZCYzqDL0

McCagh, T. (2019, November 26). *Animals & The Afterlife – Where Do They Really Go?* Animal Talk. https://www.animaltalk.com.au/animals-the-afterlife-where-do-they-really-go/

Mccagh, T. (2010). *Stories from the Animal Whisperer: What Your Pet is Thinking and Trying to Tell You.* Allen & Unwin.

Naturally Happy Dogs. (2021). *Grief and pet loss – symptoms you may experience.* In YouTube. https://www.youtube.com/watch?v=AC0_nY-z_vQ

Newton Institute. (2010). *Memories of the Afterlife: Life Between Lives Stories of Personal Transformation* (M. Newton, Ed.). Llewellyn Publications.

Oaks, S. (2022, January 18). *Man Shocked by What He Saw His Pets Doing in Heaven (Amazing NDE).* YouTube. https://www.youtube.com/watch?v=FTNdj-W0ZH4

Online, M. (2016, August 26). *After Bel Mooney revealed how her dog came to her after death, even sceptics will now ask: Can dead pets really come back to comfort their owners?* Mail Online. https://www.dailymail.co.uk/news/article-3760804/After-Bel-Mooney-revealed-dog-came-death-sceptics-ask-dead-pets-really-come-comfort-owners.html

Palmer, S. J. (1989, August). *What exactly is reincarnation? Is it contrary to the teachings of the gospel?* The Church of Jesus Christ of Latter-Day Saints.

https://abn.churchofjesuschrist.org/study/ensign/1989/08/i
-have-a-question/what-exactly-is-reincarnation-is-it-contrary-
to-the-teachings-of-the-gospel?

Parnia, S., Spearpoint, K., de Vos, G., Fenwick, P., Goldberg, D.,
Yang, J., Zhu, J., Baker, K., Killingback, H., McLean, P.,
Wood, M., Zafari, A. M., Dickert, N., Beisteiner, R., Sterz, F.,
Berger, M., Warlow, C., Bullock, S., Lovett, S., & McPara, R.
M. S. (2014). *AWARE—AWAreness during REsuscitation—A
prospective study.* Resuscitation, *85*(12), 1799–1805.
https://doi.org/10.1016/j.resuscitation.2014.09.004

Pierce, J. (2011, December 6). *Animal Heaven: What do animals do in
heaven?* Psychology Today; Sussex Publishers.
https://www.psychologytoday.com/us/blog/all-dogs-go-
heaven/201112/animal-heaven

Ragan, L. (2015). *Signs From Pets in the Afterlife: Identifying Messages
From Pets in Heaven.* Lyn Ragan.

Richardson, T. C. (2021, December 17). *A Professional Psychic On How
To Develop The 4 "Clairs" Of Intuition.* Mindfulness;
Mindbodygreen.
https://www.mindbodygreen.com/articles/the-4-types-of-
intuition-and-how-to-tap-into-each

Ring, K. (1992). *The Omega Project: Near-Death Experiences, UFO
Encounters, and Mind at Large.* William Morrow.

Robinett, K. (2018). *Tails from the Afterlife: Stories of Signs, Messages &
Inspiration from Your Animal Companions.* Llewellyn Publications.

Russell, N. (2012). *Social Zooarchaeology: Humans and Animals in
Prehistory.* Cambridge University Press.

Safina, C. (2015). *Beyond Words: What Animals Think and Feel*. Henry Holt and Company.

Sandal, V. (2018, December 15). *Animals have souls, can achieve liberation*. The Sunday Guardian Live. https://www.sundayguardianlive.com/opinion/animals-souls-can-achieve-liberation

Sheridan, K. (2009). *Animals and the Afterlife: True Stories of Our Best Friends' Journey Beyond Death*. Hay House.

Sias, J. J. (2015). *Ancient Animal Ethics: The Earliest Arguments for the Ethical Consideration of Nonhuman Animals*. The Downtown Review, *2*(1). https://doi.org/https://engagedscholarship.csuohio.edu/tdr/vol2/iss1/4

Sprankles, J. (2021, September 21). *Are You Clairsentient?* Scary Mommy. https://www.scarymommy.com/clairsentient

Stone, P. (2010). *Secrets from Beyond The Grave: The Amazing Mysteries of Eternity, Paradise, and the Land of Lost Souls*. Charisma House.

Sunfellow, D. (2019). *The Purpose of Life: As Revealed by Near-Death Experiences from Around the World*. David Sunfellow.

Thomas, C. (2003). *Heaven is so Real!* Charisma Media.

Van Lommel, P. (2010). *Consciousness Beyond Life: The Science of the Near-Death Experience*. HarperCollins.

Varghese, R. A. (2010). *There is Life After Death: Compelling Reports from Those Who Have Glimpsed the Afterlife*. New Page Books.

Vaske, T. (2017, December 22). *My dog reincarnated & came back to me?!* YouTube. https://www.youtube.com/watch?v=1Q4bsblFYVw

Wagner, T. (2006). *Thoughts and Resources About Reincarnation Reunions.* Animals in Our Hearts. https://www.animalsinourhearts.com/articles/death-afterlife/reincarnation-reunions.html

Zavada, J. (2020, April 15). *Do Animals Have Souls? Will Our Pets be in Heaven?* Learn Religions. https://www.learnreligions.com/do-animals-have-souls-701974

Printed in Great Britain
by Amazon

36979785R00076